T0165511

Back From Combat:
A World War II Bombardier Faces His Military Future

Charles N. Stevens

authorHOUSE®

AuthorHouse™
1663 Liberty Drive
Bloomington, IN 47403
www.authorhouse.com
Phone: 1-800-839-8640

First published by AuthorHouse 8/26/2011

ISBN: 978-1-4634-4266-8 (e)
ISBN: 978-1-4634-4267-5 (sc)

Library of Congress Control Number: 2011913819

Printed in the United States of America

Contents

AFTERWORD

Introduction

When I finished my combat tour with the 8th Air Force in England and was sent back to the United States, the war was still raging although the Allies seemed to be winning on all fronts.

The question for me was what am I going to do now? I am a fully trained bombardier with combat experience, but what am I good for now? I could probably get a job as a bombardier instructor, but that training program is winding down. Being an instructor does not appeal to me. I could volunteer for another tour of duty, fly bombing missions again, but being lucky enough to survive the first time, I have no motivation to do it. If there were a shortage of bombardiers, I would have no choice but to return to combat, but there are plenty of new ones to supply the Air Corps. I'm simply not needed.

After returning from overseas I was given a 30-day furlough then sent to Midland, Texas, the same field from which I graduated as a bombardier about ten months before. I became part of a large pool of veteran bombardiers and navigators. Frankly, they didn't know what to do with us. The skills we had learned were of little use anymore.

A few men who were bored, felt it was their patriotic duty, or needed danger to make them feel alive, volunteered for another tour of duty. Most of us, glad to be alive, did not feel this way. We languished at Midland with little to do, all of us wondering what our next move might be.

My furlough and now the idleness at Midland were in stark contrast to the tension and emotions of the bombing missions, living that life every day, facing death every time we went up. It was like coming off some horrible high, not quite knowing how to handle it. Plowing through an enemy anti-aircraft barrage, hoping I wouldn't be hit is nothing like watching a film about navigation in a quiet room far away from conflict.

The question, again, is what do I do now?

* * *

I wrote *An Innocent at Polebrook: A Memoir of an 8ᵗʰ Air Force Bombardier* in 2004. That book covered the ferrying of our bomber across the Atlantic to England, an account of my 34 bombing missions and my return home by ship and train. Those who read it said, "We really liked your book, but wanted more about how you were trained before going overseas." Prompted by those requests, I wrote *The Innocent Cadet: Becoming a World War II Bombardier* in 2008. This book covered classification at San Antonio, preflight at Ellington Field in Houston, Texas, aerial gunnery training in Laredo, Texas, bombardier training at

Midland, Texas and crew training on B-17s at Alexandria, Louisiana.

The word "innocent" was in both titles because I was that. I knew very little about the darker side of life, having been raised by a loving, protective family. I knew nothing of the agony of war, the astounding limits of emotion I would have to endure. I had not experienced life as much as many of the men I trained and fought with. I also looked young for my age, more like a boy than a man.

It occurred to me that my military life would be incomplete without writing about what happened to me after combat when I was still in the service and the war persisted. To fill out the story, I wrote the present book, *Back from Combat: A World War II Bombardier Faces His Military Future.* The three books complete my military life, that pivotal period that occurred so long ago when I was 18, 19, and 20. Although this is my personal story, it is also very close to the stories of many men that served in the branches of the armed forces then. I hope some men will recognize themselves in what I have written and that their families may understand more about what they went through. The war was devastating, and many young men just like me were caught up in it. This is the story of one young man who was swept into its vortex.

* * *

I was a prolific letter writer, recording my daily life in the military with accurate detail. My parents saved all my letters, tying them in bundles and storing them in a department store box. I now have all my letters, their contents supplying the stories and details found in my books. My memories of the time are still vivid, and the emotional content of them help hold the facts together. As one might imagine, some of my experiences did not find their way into my letters, but are still firmly lodged in my memory.

I have written all my books in present tense to make the story more immediate, to take the reader along with me. I also wrote it from a first person point of view, again to bring the reader close to me. Whereas the chapters are generally chronological, they are not strictly so, some of the chapters being built around themes. Near the end of the book they are strictly chronological.

Where I felt it was appropriate I quoted passages directly from my letters. These are always set apart and typed in italics. I either wanted to make a point with them or to demonstrate the language of an 18 or 19 year old boy/ man who never liked his English classes. The irony is that I became an English teacher.

I have included an afterword to my book composed of stories outside the scope of *Back from Combat*, but related to my experiences in World War II.

The book is written from the view point of the young man I was then---but by an 86 year-old man. Experience, education, circumstances and living have altered how I feel and what I think over the years. I'm not as innocent as I was then, but in many ways I am still like that young man.

* * *

As I stressed in my other books, I believe it is important to write things down, to have some record of having lived.

Otherwise, when a person dies, he fades away, disappears from the earth, gradually passes out of the memory of those who follow. Rain and wind obliterate names on tombstones. Future generations will not know anything about that life. He will only be a name on a genealogical chart without the knowledge of the life he led---his unique experiences, what he liked and didn't like, what made him happy or sad, what made him feel alive and what didn't. People unborn today will want to know about those who came before them.

I don't write just about war and the military. I enjoy writing about my childhood and events that have happened all through my life---even my life at 86. I am no more important than anybody else, but I have a yearning to let those who follow me know who I was as a human being. It is my little mark on the earth, my bitty smidgen of immortality.

* * *

When I was discharged from the service in October of 1945, I enrolled at UCLA, using the GI Bill to pay for tuition and financial support. The training I received in the service gave me confidence that I could succeed at the university. I was now more motivated and more skilled at studying.

I graduated with a degree in psychology with minors in sociological and biological sciences. I remained at UCLA an extra year to earn my teaching credential.

I worked briefly as a science teacher at Dinuba, California then moved on to Barstow, California where I taught for two years. I became a science teacher in

Montebello, California where I continued to teach for 31 years. After earning a master's degree in English at California State College I switched from science to English, ending my career by teaching American Literature at Schurr High School in Montebello. I retired in 1984 and have spent my time reading, writing, traveling and bonding with my grandchildren.

I married in 1948 and had two sons, Jeffry Lowell Stevens and Greg Eric Stevens. I have five grandchildren---Brenda Stevens Sherry , Sharon Stevens, Eric Stevens , Michael Stevens and Beth Stevens. I now have two great grandchildren, Ryan and Colin Stevens.

I remarried in 1972 to Dolores Seidman. We have had 39 wonderful years together, and she is affectionately known as Grandma Dee to our grandchildren.

First of all I would like to thank my wife, Dolores Seidman, for her enthusiasm about my books and for her sharp-eyed editing skills. Without her patience and encouragement the books would not have been written.

I appreciate the help preparing the photographs for the book given by my son, Jeffry Stevens.

I would also like to thank the Wordknot Writing Group---Davin Malasarn (our leader), Marie Shield, Maggie Malooly, Frances O'Brien, Alice Hayward, Sue Coppa and John Young---who read and listened to every chapter of this book and provided many valuable suggestions.

Charles "Norm" Stevens
Monterey Park, California

A Return to Midland

I lean back in my Pullman seat, gazing out at the vast desert of gravel and scrawny mesquite under an arid blue sky. Now and then the train passes rocky outcrops that resemble fields strewn with broken pottery. After my thirty-day furlough at home I'm much more relaxed, maybe even a bit lazy. The constant rhythm of the wheels ticking over the rails lulls me into a sleepy reverie.

Rolling across west Texas on a Southern Pacific train reminds me of the time, over a year ago, when I was on my way to San Antonio to begin cadet training. It seems so long ago. Since then I had gone through months of study and conditioning, aerial gunnery and bombardier training, preparation for combat with a heavy bomber crew and had survived thirty-four bombing missions in Europe.

Back then the adventure was all ahead of me. All of that excitement, apprehension and curiosity was yet to come. Now it's all behind me, all those emotions having faded into dreams and memories. I've completed a cycle,

1

but the war still rages, and what my next assignment will be is a mystery. What will I do? I don't want to return for another tour in England.

I think about my leave, a whole month doing just what I wanted, no one giving me orders. It was wonderful being in Inglewood again, nestling in the bosom of my family. Being there seemed so natural--- my mother in the kitchen cooking on the old Acorn stove, my dad coming home from work, tramping through the back porch with his lunchbox, my dog curled up asleep on the floor, quivering in his dreams. The house was just as I had left it. How I had longed for it those many months! But I was not the same boy who left it over a year before.

I slept late and did almost nothing to help around the house. I had no motivation for anything except being there, being safe and away from the war and the rigors of the army. At first I tried to tell my family about my combat experiences, the stories that lay bottled up in my mind all these months. They listened, but I could read the expression on their faces, a faraway look that told me they couldn't comprehend them. I knew they couldn't completely understand, but I told them anyway because I needed to.

I remember one incident with my father. I wore the ribbon for the Distinguished Flying Cross on my uniform, a medal I had earned by completing my thirty gut-wrenching missions.

"How did you earn that medal?" he asked.

"It was awarded to me for enduring thirty bombing missions."

"There must be more to it than that. You can tell me. What exactly did you get it for?"

"I did nothing specifically heroic except for having the courage to face the hell of all those bombing raids."

"Well I'm sure you did more than that. I think you're just being modest."

I could never convince him. Plainly he had no idea of the terrifying ordeals I had been through. If he had, he would understand why I received the medal. Furthermore, he would continue believing his son was a hero in the Hollywood sense, that I had done something special like sacrificing my safety or risking my life for the welfare of others.

I tried to tell my girlfriend about my experiences, but she looked blankly into space, as though her mind was full of other thoughts. She plainly didn't want to hear about them as they were too far removed from her sheltered life. I gave her a small chunk of flak that had lodged in our wing during an afternoon raid on Rouen, France. It was a memento I innocently thought she might like. But to her it must have seemed only a jagged lump of metal. Puzzled, she looked at it briefly then thanked me as though she didn't know what else to do. To me the sharp piece of shrapnel was a reminder of a withering anti-aircraft barrage, one that knocked a plane down that was flying close to us, one that drove cold fear deep into my bones.

I knew my parents sensed I was different now, that they had to get used to this new person. The innocent landscape of my mind was now strewn with strange and grotesque images, black visions of combat and the coarseness of men. How could I be the same?

I had visited areas of my emotions that I had never known before. They had been stretched to their limit. I had known fear before but never the dry-mouthed, numbing, intestinal extent of it I had felt on the missions when death was always a distinct possibility. On the other hand I had soared to new heights of euphoria when, returning from missions, I saw the English Channel ahead and knew I was going to be safe.

I was more serious and somber now but at loose ends, not knowing what to do with myself. At the same time, having dodged death overseas, I had a new appreciation of life.

While on leave I remember seeing a man running for a bus, shouting for the driver to wait. Not hearing the man, the driver sped away in a cloud of exhaust. The running man stopped, cursing the driver and his bad luck. He stalked away muttering to himself. I wondered why the man was so upset about such a trivial matter. He had his life didn't he? He was not injured or bleeding. Maybe I should have sympathized more with him, but I was so glad to be alive that nothing else seemed important.

Some time around midnight I wake up in my Pullman upper berth violently sick at my stomach. Waves of nausea ripple through my belly. I retch and foul my upper berth before I can get out of it. It must have been the seafood dinner I'd consumed in the diner. The porter kindly cleans up the berth then allows me to sleep on a cushioned bench in the men's room. I doze off at times but often need to dash to the bathroom. My abdominal muscles cramp to the point that I think I'm breaking in two.

It's still dark when we approach Midland early in the morning. I struggle into my uniform and gather my heavy barracks bag. When the train stops at Midland, my coach is at least a quarter mile from the station. I jump down from the steps onto the rocky ballast at the side of the rails, the freezing December air cutting into my face. Still weak from my ordeal on the train, I head toward the station, the footing treacherous, my bag banging against my legs. Up ahead, the steam from the locomotive curls around the station flood lights.

Exhausted by the time I reach the platform, I shuffle into the warmth of the waiting room. I telephone the air base then stretch out on one of the hard polished benches, waiting to be picked up. I'm homesick already.

A staff car arrives and shuttles me to the field. I report for duty then walk over to the flight surgeon's office where the doctor gives me some Amphogel to settle my stomach. I recover quickly.

I learn that our courses here at Midland will be mostly review and that classes will not start for five more days. This will give me a chance to get some flying time, essential if I want to receive my flight pay. I would have time to get back into the Air Force routine again, its strict regulation of my life.

Adjustments

By hitching rides on AT-11s with bombardier trainees, I'd accumulated seven hours of my required twelve to receive flight pay. The last time I'd been in the air was my final bombing mission, a raid on the Land Armament Works at Kassel, Germany. That mission was only two months ago, yet already it's like a vague dream or a distant memory. That raid, as well as all the others, is steeped in an aura of unreality, as though I'd only imagined it. The missions were so intense, so vastly different from ordinary experience that they now seem strangely unreal.

Flying in AT-11s again after so many months in overloaded B-17s is quite a contrast. B-17s burdened with bombs and full fuel tanks used nearly all the runway to become airborne while the flimsy twin-engine AT-11s take up only half of it, leaping into the air like grasshoppers. The light planes bounce and buck in the air currents. I have to get used to their erratic jerks and jolts again, but flying without a care, not having to scan the sky for enemy fighter planes or enduring anti-aircraft barrages is relaxing. But I have to admit that sometimes, out of habit, I catch myself looking for them.

The view from the plane's nose is different now, the scene shifting from the emerald green fields, rolling hills and fresh rivers of England to the dry brush-stippled plains and sandy washes of Texas. Flying over English forests, the mosaics of fields, hedgerows and picturesque villages was always a pleasure. Now I have to get used to seeing the arid expanse of west Texas again.

I catch a ride with a long navigation mission, a great opportunity to increase my flight time. I'm surprised to see that the two students are black, and so is the first lieutenant who is also taking the course. The Army Air Corps is strictly segregated, so it's unusual to see black cadets. These men are navigating well, hitting their cities right on the nose. I practice pilotage navigation on my own, checking landmarks against my maps. I feel better when I know exactly where I am.

* * *

Homesickness had set in again as soon as my train left Los Angeles Union Station for Midland, and grows stronger each day.

I love California and Inglewood more than any other place on earth. I want to get back there and stay.

During my leave I had simply vegetated, allowing my parents to take care of me again, as though I were their boy once more.

I should have gotten up early with you guys...I sure

appreciated all you did for me while I was at home. I'm afraid I wasn't very helpful. They say combat makes you lazy. I guess they were right.

I was exhausted, the difficulty of training and the tension of the bombing missions sapping my energy. Perhaps I'd been worn down more than I thought, as long sleeps at night and into the day felt luscious and healing. Maybe I just wanted to feel safe again, slumbering like a child in my own bed, home being the most secure place I could imagine.

* * *

One delight about returning to Midland is being reacquainted with men I had known there before going overseas. Most of all I enjoy seeing Captain Cannady again. Then-Lieutenant Cannady had been my first bombsight instructor, the one who taught me the basics on the "oil derrick" trainers, the contraptions that crept across the floor guided by the bombardier trainee to a target marked on a little "stool" across the room. He firmly shakes my hand.

"Welcome back. I'm happy to see you again," he says. "Where did you go when you left here?"

"I trained on B-17s at Alexandria, Louisiana then went overseas to England and the 8th Air Force. I flew with the 351st Bomb Group."

"Well you've really been through it. Happy you survived all that."

He's the only superior officer I personally respected. He was genuinely interested in his students, sensitive to how they felt. Many officers appeared to enjoy their exalted status, often lording it over others, savoring their power. Lieutenant Cannady recognized that regardless of rank we were all human beings and that we should treat each other as such. His easygoing style was perfect for me, and I learned quickly from him. He did insist that I call him Sir, not that he cared, but as he said, "You better get used to calling me Sir because some chicken shit officer will rack you back if you don't." Sure enough, it did happen to me later.

I also run into my former instructor from Alexandria and another man who had been in my preflight class at Ellington Field as well as my aerial gunnery class at Laredo. He finished his tour with the 15th Air Force in Italy. I bump into a few more men who were in my bombardier class and my group overseas. Meeting these men again helps assuage my homesickness.

* * *

The base commander informs us that we'll have five hours of ground school navigation every day plus more training on the autopilot and the bombsight. The program will also include PT (physical training). I hadn't exercised much since finishing cadet training. During our overseas duty we were too exhausted and concerned about the missions to even think about it. But I welcome it. I know I'm out of shape, my muscles flabby, my abdomen beginning to creep over my belt.

I'm disappointed with the food in our mess halls, its quality having deteriorated since my cadet days. The cooks have the ingredients, but they don't prepare meals with any skill or imagination.

It's sure inferior to that swell food you cooked for me while I was at home…We had powdered eggs scrambled this morning. The only thing that reminded me of eggs is that they were yellow.

Winter

During the night ice coated the base, encasing roofs and walks, twigs and even blades of grass. The winter setting is magical, its beauty a rare sight. I stand at the barracks window admiring the cold glittering scene. Later, a steady rain melts it all away, but it's striking while it lasts.

The following morning a thick fog obscures the barracks around us, transforming them into silent rectangular ghosts. The cold, clammy mist sends chills through my bones. When the fog thins it leaves a haze that dulls everything, even my outlook on life.

One of our AT-11s crashes in the desert, a victim of the weather, the pilot apparently trying to get under a low ceiling. Three cadets and two officers are killed. I didn't know any of them, yet I feel for them and think about flying, all that can happen to us. I imagine the twisted wreckage, the broken bodies of the men. I should know by now that accidents are part of flying, that it always has been risky business. Young men plus complex machines in addition to the vagaries of weather are a potential lethal mix.

The incident reminds me of my cadet days here in Midland when we lost a plane at night, killing three cadets and two pilots. It was grim business assembling for a roll call afterwards to confirm who had been killed. One of them was a friend of mine, a funny guy, full of life, who made everyone laugh. It was the first time I seriously thought that something like this could actually happen.

Despite the beastly weather, I get in my last hour of required flying time to qualify for flight pay.

Later, several of us from the barracks ignore the wet, icy footing to see a movie called "The Three Caballeros," a standard movie combined with cartoon characters.

* * *

Letters and packages trickle in from home, one from my Aunt Mary and my grandmother containing a new cribbage board and a handkerchief. I have yet to receive Christmas gifts from my folks.

My girlfriend sends me a picture of herself, but no letter. In the previous one she had taken me to task for the way I treated her on my leave, when I told her I was also seeing someone else. I'll not write her until I get another letter from her.

The days roll by, but she doesn't write. It hurts. If she doesn't write soon, I'll know something's up.

Well I'm not going to worry about it. If it goes on the rocks this time, I won't have anything to do with her again. She

really messed it up once before, but she won't do it again. Maybe
that is pretty harsh, but that's the way I feel about it now.

A letter from her finally arrives, cheering me up. It's like a warm, bright light burrowing through the fog, evaporating my hostile attitude toward her.

* * *

I meet one of my old classmates, Jerry Fox.

"Hey! Nice to see you again, Stevens. It's been a long time."

"Yeah it has," I answer. "I still remember that bivouac out in the boonies when we were cadets. There were two other guys in the tent with us. I had frost on my shoes when we got up in the morning. I remember how cold and stiff they were when I stuck my feet in them."

"I remember that too. Smith and Withers were the other two guys. Smith was killed in action and Withers had to bail out coming home from a mission."

"My God! I'm sorry about them."

"That's not the worst of it. Seven guys from our bombardier class all went to the same group. Only one got back alive. That guy was involved in a mid-air collision and had to bail out. The accident screwed up his mind and they grounded him."

"That's horrible."

"I'm sorry to be the bearer of bad news, but that's the way it is."

"Do you remember Glenn Ballentyne?" I asked. "He was in our cadet class at Midland. He's the only one from our class that wound up with the 351st Bomb Group with me. I was flying near him; I think it was just after we had bombed the Naval Yards at Kiel, Germany, when one of their engines caught fire. The pilot put the plane into a steep dive, I assume, to blow out the fire. They dove straight down, the plane blazing like a torch. It disappeared down in the haze. Later I learned that they had to bail out and became prisoners of war."

"Yeah, I remember him. Nice guy."

Every day I hear about the fate of my former friends. One man that I knew, a big, strong guy was hit in the head with a taut spring from a machine gun. Somehow the incident pushed him over a psychological edge, and he was also grounded. Someone told me about Sachs too. "Oh, he went down," said an officer. And then I pictured him in my mind, the way he slept, his head on his pillow, his puffy cheeks reminding me of a cherub. Now he's gone too. Every time I hear these reports, I become more aware of how lucky I was, never being shot down or injured. We lost thirty-one planes from our field while I was at Polebrook but sheer luck and circumstance kept me whole.

The temperature is always below freezing in the morning, the ground covered with thick frost looking much like a light snowfall. I admire the raw beauty of it, but the sharp edge of the polar air cuts clear through me. It's like my life, my desire for new experiences, thoughts of home and possible furloughs, against the backdrop of bleak loneliness, homesickness, the loss of friends and apprehensions about the next step in my military life.

Options

━━━━━━━━━━

The Commanding Officer gives us four options to choose from after completing our training here at Midland, all of them, unfortunately, eventually leading back to combat.

The first is volunteering for another tour of duty as a bombardier in England or Italy. Obviously, having just returned from combat I have no desire to plunge back into that aerial cesspool. I was lucky enough to get through it all the first time.

The second is to be sent to Selman Field, Louisiana for celestial navigation training. Upon completion of this course I would be sent overseas as a full fledged navigator.

The third "opportunity" would be attending a BTO (Bombing Through the Overcast) school, which would include learning about radar sets and using them to navigate and locate bombing targets. Again, I would have to agree for a tour of duty in the Pacific on B-29s.

The last option would be becoming an instructor in

the Training Command until they found a place to use me overseas.

I decide on BTO school as my first choice with Training Command second.

I have to admit that I'm intrigued with the Boeing B-29, that it holds a certain fascination for me. Its immense size and power stokes my imagination. During one of our classes we see a film about the craft. It's a massive plane, so large and heavy that it requires a longer runway than the B-17. A friend who has flown in B-29s tells me that the pilot waits until he has attained ninety-five miles per hour then pulls back on the control column and just waits for the plane to take off.

As a B-29 base at Pyote, Texas is only about fifty miles from Midland, the big silver birds often fly over or near our field. They're huge, their shiny aluminum bulk glinting in the sun, and I'm curious to know what it's like to fly in one.

Once, out of curiosity, we fly down to Pyote during a training mission, circle their field and gawk at the Superfortresses below. They're more than impressive, their gargantuan bodies and wings casting great shadows on the concrete flight line. I know that the course I have chosen will eventually lead me to this plane.

I'm concerned that my decision will worry my folks, but perhaps the war will be over by the time I finish my training. It's a gamble.

You know I hope you are not worried about the choice I made. I think you have always liked the idea of me becoming an instructor. In this choice I considered only myself, and it's hard, but that's about all you can do in the Air Corps. As much as I hate even the thought of combat or anything connected with it, I'm afraid I'm not going to settle down until after the war. I trust and have faith in God and believe that he will guide me in all that I do.

* * *

A late Christmas package from home finally arrives after being lost in transit for over a week. In it is a good pen, fresh handkerchiefs, dates and icebox cookies. The cookies are crisp, as though they had just been baked. I love my mother's icebox cookies. She would mix the dough and form it into a small loaf then place it in the icebox to cool and become firm. Later she would cut quarter inch slices from the loaf and place them on a cookie sheet to bake. The sweet fragrance of the baking cookies would fill the house. To have a warm one right out of the oven was heaven. Even the raw dough, when she would give us a little bite, was tasty. When the cookies cooled she placed them in a tin box that was always out on the table.

Tasting and smelling the cookies now takes me back home to the time when I was a carefree boy who knew nothing of the tensions of war, to a place where I was safe and people loved me.

* * *

As it is Sunday I attend church services as I always do, then take in a movie, "Experiment Perilous" with Heddy Lamar, George Brent and Paul Lucas.

Also at the movie theater a bombardier from my squadron at Polebrook and I see a recent "March of Time." We're surprised to see one about the 8th Air Force and even more amazed to see shots of our own field. One especially is of our briefing room complete with the curtains and the large map. We know it was our field because our insignias were on their leather jackets. Most of the photos of planes were from Molesworth, the nearby base of the 303rd Bomb Group. The briefing room seemed like a person I had known once. Seeing a place that had meant so much to me, now being viewed by thousands of people in theaters was exciting.

Johnston, the pilot of our crew overseas, writes me a brief letter. He's at the Laredo Army Air Base flying B-17s for gunners. When they are "attacked" by fighter planes they use camera guns to "shoot them down." They also shoot real bullets at sleeve targets pulled by other planes.

Our first required flight at Midland is a 200-mile navigation mission. I navigate by dead reckoning. I don't look out the window to check my position with landmarks. I plan the course with a compass, air speed indicator, temperature gauge, dividers, pencil, watch and my E6B Computer. I miss my destination city by two miles and my ETA by two minutes.

* * *

Some pilots flying at Midland are sloppy, a danger to everyone who flies with them. On one of our flights, while heading east, another plane approaches us coming from the north. It's only about two hundred yards away and appears to be headed straight for us. Neither pilot appears to be trying to evade the other. Within seconds the plane passes beneath us, missing us by only a few feet. My mouth is wide open and my heart flips. I climb out of the nose to see what the pilot is doing. The idiot has the plane on autopilot and is engrossed in writing a letter. He didn't even see the other plane. We all work him over verbally after we land.

"You could've killed us all up there," shouts one of the cadets.

"Well, nothing happened did it? The other guy probably saw me. I think it just looked close," replies the pilot.

"Yeah, well you could watch out where you're goin'."

Besides this near mishap he had run out of fuel three times before he switched tanks, making our engines sputter and giving us fits of panic when we began losing altitude. He also took off much too close behind another plane that tossed us around in its prop wash and could have twisted us into the runway.

I receive a letter from Perry Smith, one of my high school friends, who is a bombardier-navigator on an A-26 attack bomber with the 9th Air Force. Every friend of mine is in one branch of the service or another. Such is life for anyone my age during wartime.

Christmas

The base commander announces that we'll have two days off for Christmas. I'd like to go home, but the only way I can get there is by flying, and that's out of the question. I don't have enough money or time. Perhaps I could take a trip on my own to El Paso. I was impressed with its tall buildings when we passed through on the train, but I don't know anyone there. Midland or Odessa, several miles to our west are uninspiring. I consider traveling to Abilene, but I don't know anything about the town, and being there would only intensify my loneliness. I remember being by myself in other cities like Galveston and Salt Lake City and how isolated I felt being among strangers who knew each other but didn't know me, the doors of businesses and stores closed on weekends, locked up tight, shutting me out, nothing but gray metal emptiness.

I think about Christmas at home, the intoxicating fragrance of the fir tree all through the house. I can imagine the scent now, the gathering around the tree on

Christmas morning, earlier than my parents would have liked. I see the wrapped packages in the dim light of the colored bulbs strung on the tree. I hear the sound of paper ripping, impatient hands busy. But it's not the gifts I care about now; it's being there with the delicate silhouette of the tree on the wall, the soft splashes of color from the lights, the voices of my family.

I'm not a kid anymore, but that's what's on my mind, and I'm going to sorely miss a wonderful time. The frost coating the ground and the nose-numbing nip in the morning air intensifies my visions of Christmas.

I decide to stay in the barracks during our days off and catch up on my correspondence. My memories will have to substitute for a real Christmas at home.

* * *

In contrast to the Christmas spirit drifting through the base, the commanding officers, for reasons I don't understand, forbid us to wear our leather jackets. Perhaps it's because most men who wear them have been in combat, some of the jackets still carrying the name of their bomb group or plane. I admit that some of the jackets are a bit worn and raunchy and maybe not up to military standards, but we cherish them. They want all of us to be the same without one group standing out against another. I mutter to myself about these Scrooges.

*Ground Grippers, Swivel Chair Jockeys, Paddlefeet…..
These guys and their rules.*

Our treatment differs markedly from the lax attitude

that was tolerated overseas. As long as we performed our jobs, the general rules of conduct were overlooked.

Another rule the commanders dream up is that we must wear our gas masks all day on Mondays. I can understand making us do this in cadet training when they were trying to instill discipline, but requiring us to wear them now seems unnecessary. I suppose they're trying to stiffen the rules for those of us who are back from overseas and are used to a more permissive atmosphere. But it feels like punishment to the combat veterans who have recently risked their lives. Possibly they're jealous of us. The masks are exceedingly uncomfortable, made warm and sticky from the condensation of our breaths.

* * *

I'm happy about receiving a letter from Jack Podoske, the co-pilot on our overseas crew and my best friend. It's like receiving a Christmas present. I had immediately liked Jack at our first crew training meeting at Alexandria. We often went to the movies or town together. Overseas the two of us traveled to London then journeyed to Scotland for a week-long flak leave. Taller than I and handsome with his thick wavy hair, he had a sparkling personality. He lit up one cigarette after another and loved a cold glass of beer or a shot of bourbon. Even though I didn't share his habits, we got along well.

On our thirtieth mission, a raid on the I.G. Farben chemical plant at Ludwigshaven, Germany, a chunk of flak penetrated deep into his thigh. At the time he didn't know where he was hit or how far the shrapnel had dug into his body. He thought for awhile that it had reached his intestines, or worse, his groin. We got him into the navigator and bombardier's compartment where he lay still but conscious, his flying suit ripped and bloody.

After our crew completed our thirty-four missions and left the airfield at Polebrook, Podoske was still in the base hospital. This letter is the first word from him I have had since leaving Polebrook. He's up and around now but his leg is still sore and partially numb. They gave him a thorough physical examination then grounded him for three months. Still at the field, he's waiting for division headquarters to decide whether they should send him home or require him to finish his remaining four missions.

Our ball turret gunner, Kellogg, was told to finish his final thirteen missions when the rest of us had finished ours. He had become our ball turret gunner after our original one, Santo Caruso, was severely injured by flak on our third mission. Caruso who was in the hospital during the rest of our tour had finally been released from it and is now flying with another crew. I'm glad Caruso was okay as he was a funny little guy who always joked around and kept up our spirits.

* * *

Our review classes start with a dull, black and white film, monotonously narrated, about the autopilot, followed by a class on altitude computation. We endure calisthenics in the freezing air then run a half mile, our breaths puffing and steaming. In the afternoon we sit through five hours of navigation classes.

At night we have movies at the base theater, helping to entertain us and keep us from becoming bored. Tonight we see "The Belle of the Yukon" starring Randolph Scott, Dinah Shore, Gypsy Rose Lee and Bob Burns. It is just the kind of film that takes my mind off unpleasant matters.

"Silent Night," "Hark the Herald Angles Sing" and "Joy to the World" drift out of the radio all day long, increasing my longing for home. Christmas is going to be trying for all of us cooped up here with no place to go.

But I'm back in the United States and in one piece. Asking for more would be greedy.

The wind is icy and the clouds low and gray with a promise of snow. I wear my trench coat everywhere outside, buttoning it up around my neck, just under my chin. It's Christmas weather, making me both happy and unhappy. Because of the chilly weather they call off calisthenics as a kind of holiday gift.

I learn that my Grandmother Stevens is ill and confined to her bed. She's quite old, very conservative, religious and puritanical, but I love her very much. She concocts the most delicious fig jam on earth and prepares magnificent roast beef dinners with roasted potatoes and buckets of rich brown gravy.

* * *

Christmas Eve church services make me think even more about home. The subdued service is far removed from the commotion in the barracks afterwards. Almost everyone is drunk except me. I suppose they sing and yell out of loneliness and boredom, most of them wishing they were home. If I were a drinking man, I'd be drunk too. A group of intoxicated carolers tromp into our room then perform their alcoholic rendition of "Silent Night," their words slurred, loud and off key, whisky vapors on their breaths perfuming our quarters. I grin and laugh at them as they're having a hell of a good time.

* * *

I attend Christmas Day church services with two men I'd trained with at Ellington field. Both had been sent to the 15th Air Force in Italy. One had finished his tour while the other one was shot down on his third mission, a dangerous low-level raid to the Ploesti Oil Fields in Romania. He somehow escaped from the Germans and made his way back to Italy. We're all thankful we're back in the United States and are still whole.

* * *

Christmas has passed, and now I can forget about it. The days will be like any other. Winter has locked the base in its grip. Rain patters on the roof, but the temperature is below thirty-two degrees, the drops freezing as they hit, covering everything with ice. It's spectacular to look out upon it, but we have to be careful not to slip and fall on our asses when we go out. It's beautiful, but treacherous.

Riding with the Avengers

Finishing up at Midland, I'm sent to Selman Field at Monroe, Louisiana. After only a few days, I'm given a leave and seize a great opportunity that drops right out of the sky.

* * *

The planes circle into Selman field like an orderly flock of bluebirds, a squadron of them, deep blue like the color of the open sea. The Navy TBM Avengers taxi down the flight line, park wing to wing on the ramp. Avengers are rare at Selman Field where Beechcraft AT-7 navigation trainers dominate. The torpedo bombers appear powerful and poised as they rest on the tarmac, the pilots and observers sliding back their canopies and climbing out of their cockpits. A few already walk toward the operations office.

I strike up a conversation with one of the pilots.

"Where are you guys going?"

"We're staying here tonight then we'll be on our way to the west coast, San Francisco."

"Are you flying non-stop?"

"No. We'll fly to Abilene, Texas tomorrow then on to Phoenix, Palm Springs and San Francisco."

"I've got a leave coming. Any chance of tagging along with you as far as Palm Springs?"

"I don't know. You'll have to clear it with the squadron leader."

I finally locate their leader, a friendly officer who gives his okay. I have to clear the trip with the field, requisition a parachute and report to the planes at 0900.

"There's a compartment down below where you can ride. It's not very comfortable, but it'll get you there."

"Great. Another guy and I will see you at 0900 with our parachutes."

The following morning Jim, a navigator, and I walk out to the planes carrying our back pack chutes and a small traveling bag. The closer we approach the planes, the larger they loom. Beneath the plane are the bays where they carry torpedoes, and just aft of those is a hatch door leading to the compartment where I'll ride. I'll have a port hole and a small window to look out of. Inside is a jump seat and seat belt, the interior of the chamber basic aluminum ribs and skin.

I slide into the seat, buckle up, ready to go. The powerful radial engine coughs into life, its roar and vibrations filling my compartment. We taxi slowly out to the runway and wheel into position. The pilot revs the engine up to full power, his brakes set. He suddenly releases them. We surge down the runway, intense pressure on my back. Quickly we become airborne, pointing steeply skyward. It's the kind of takeoff they perform on aircraft carriers. After lumbering down the full runway in loaded B-17s, this sensation is like taking off in a rocket.

The Avengers fly in loose formation at only a thousand feet, sometimes even lower. The view from my window is perfect as we race across the flatlands with every feature below clear and close up.

At one point my pilot takes our plane down until we're only a few hundred feet over a railroad track. We catch up with a passenger train streaking west, our plane over the coaches. I don't know what the people on the train think about seeing us so close. We pass the locomotive, a mixture of steam and rich black smoke rolling back from its stack laying down over the coaches and right of way. What a sight! We never did anything quite like this in B-17s or AT-11s.

We fly so low over small towns that we can easily read their names lettered on their silver water towers. Houses, streets and trees flash by.

I can only remember flying very low once in B-17s when our whole group flew a few hundred feet off the deck over the liberated portion of France. Farmers waved at us and bomb craters filled with muddy water gaped like great sores. Our oxygen system had been damaged by flak, so we were relieved to be at that low level.

We land at Abilene, Texas and stay in a hotel overnight. I find the navy men lively and friendly, a joy to be with. We share observations about the flight, and they ask me questions about my combat duty. Jim, the navigator traveling with me, is reticent, avoiding the men and remaining quiet. When he speaks, his voice is weak. He tells me he's uncomfortable with the men, that he feels inferior to them as they are navy pilots brimming with vitality, so opposite from his personality. I can't understand why he belittles himself. He's a decorated navigator with over thirty combat bombing missions to his credit. He knows what it's like to fly through anti-aircraft fire and suffer the apprehensions of a real mission. These navy men had never seen action, don't know what it's like. He had had vastly more experience than they. Surely his shyness runs deeper than the reasons he gives.

We take off the next morning. It's exciting to leap from the runway again. It's like taking a thrill ride at the Pomona Fair. We fly low again while the land is level, but gain altitude to top the mountains of New Mexico. We're close to the peaks, many of them above the timberline, the bald rock dappled with snow.

I think about these untested men, what lies ahead of them. Although they never tell me exactly where they're going, they know they'll be drawn into the Pacific War, perhaps on a carrier leaving California for the battle zone. I think that's why they're so lively now with their laughter, patter and jokes. Along with the natural bubbling of youth, the specter of future combat must weigh on their minds, and all the frivolity is a way of masking it, keeping it at bay. I saw the same pre-combat hilarity when my own crew went overseas. Being only twenty years old myself, I feel a kinship with these men. We're all swept into the war together, but in different ways. We carry the same unspoken doubts and apprehensions.

We land at the Litchfield Navy Base in Phoenix, Arizona where we stay for the night. The following afternoon we make the short hop from Phoenix to Palm Springs. I wish the men good luck and say good bye. Jim and I go our different ways.

An officer on the base gives me a lift into town, letting me off at Highway 111. I stand by the side of the road as the sun sets trying to hail a ride. Finally, a woman stops and offers me a lift to Los Angeles. She's young, but older than I am, perhaps twenty-five or even thirty. It's nearly dark, and deep shadows soften her face. We talk very little as we drive west, asking only a few questions of one another. She lets me off in downtown Los Angeles. It's good to be in the city with the lights, theaters, traffic and streetcars. I catch the familiar "5" car, taking it all the way to Inglewood, my home town. A short bus ride will get me home.

Back to Louisiana

Sitting comfortably in a plush Pullman seat on Santa Fe's California Limited, I'm on my way back to Selman field. I still bask in the warmth of my leave and the thrill of riding with the Navy torpedo planes.

Near Flagstaff, Arizona I gaze out of the train window at a thin veneer of patchy snow beneath the pine trees. I enjoy its cold beauty, but a persistent sadness, like the scabby earth between the patches, is with me. Even though I'm still humming inside with thoughts about my leave, I'm still in the service, the war still rages, and I'm off to a new place---more strangeness, more sterile barracks, more men I don't know, more uncertainty.

As the train races through open country, the other service men and some of the young civilians begin to bond. Several men strike up conversations then include others, the camaraderie spreading through the coach like a chemical reaction. We are all traveling to different destinations, facing the same unknowns. What fuses us into instant comradeship is what we have in common.

Across the aisle is another bombardier, a man I had trained with at Ellington Field and Laredo. I don't know him very well, but we find we have much to talk about---the men we once knew and what happened to them, our experiences overseas. Thoughts about home and hearth gradually fade, overshadowed by the chatter of wartime brotherhood.

A thin frosting of snow blankets the ground as we approach Kansas City. We roll into the station on time at 2030 hours. After purchasing my ticket for the following day, I walk through the cavernous, echoing station then out into the frigid air for a taxi. At 2100 I'm about ready for bed in my room at the luxurious Hotel Continental.

Arriving at the station early the next morning, I devour a breakfast of fried eggs, potatoes and sausage in its cozy restaurant, the fragrance of fresh coffee and hot grease heavy in the air. Afterwards I walk out into the bustle of the station---passengers dashing for trains, the echoing loudspeakers announcing departures. I'm ready for the next adventure.

I push my way onto Missouri Pacific's "Southerner," a first-rate train that will take me as far as Little Rock, Arkansas. After an all-day trip, it chugs into the Little Rock station at 2300. Since the train for Monroe is not scheduled to leave until 0245, I have a four hour layover with no place to lie down.

Two sailors I met on the train and I decide to walk into town just to be doing something. All the shops are closed, and the streets empty except for an occasional passing car, the pale light from street lamps casting eerie shadows. The only sounds are those of our voices and the muted scuffling of our shoes on the sidewalk

In this cemetery-like quietness and sterile streets we happen upon an all night diner, its lights spilling out into the chill air, like a jewel against black velvet. In its warmth and brightness we order tall glasses of milk and wedges of apple pie, eating and drinking slowly to extend our stay. The sweetness of the apples spiced with cinnamon, the flaky crust "hit the spot."

Satisfied, we walk back to the station where we discover a section we had overlooked, a small lounge area sponsored by the Red Cross. I sink into an easy chair with the intention of writing a letter, but my eyelids are heavy.

The train for Monroe finally arrives, but sleeping or weary passengers fill every seat. I stand in the aisle or sometimes in the noisy vestibule at the end of the coach, hoping people will detrain at one of the stations. Only after we've traveled 150 miles do I finally find an open seat. The train reminds me of those in and out of London where we had to push our way through the crowds trying to board it then hustle to find a seat.

The only pleasant part of the tiresome journey is a conversation with a sailor I met on the train down from Kansas City. He's on furlough after six months duty on an aircraft carrier and is returning to his home in Monroe. He's married and has a family, but he's still in the Navy. He says, "I have three of the best sons in all the world." I admire him for the love he expresses for his children. He goes on to say, "We got married when I was nineteen, and we've been happily married for over seven years." I listen with interest and a touch of awe. He embodies what I've always wanted, but seems so far away; a bonding with a woman I could love who would love me in return, then children growing out of that love who are in turn loved---like the family I came from. I yearn to duplicate that pattern in my life. He invites me over to his house for a chicken dinner, if we can get together.

I imagine myself sitting with his family around their dining room table---his wife gracious, the boys with greasy fingers and lips gnawing happily on plump drumsticks, an aura of love and the spicy smell of fried chicken all about us.

Much Ado about Nothing

═══════════

I'm assigned to the Redeployment Training Center at Selman Field at Monroe, Louisiana. Its function is to train us then parcel us out elsewhere. The elsewhere for me will be Langley Field, Virginia for Bombing Through the Overcast (BTO) training---dropping bombs by means of radar. The training here at Selman Field is whatever the staff can dream up to fill our time and keep us from being idle. How long I'll have to wait for redeployment is unknown. The school at Langley wants fresh new bombardiers who have just graduated for the BTO courses, accepting only a few veterans at approximately two-week intervals. I could be here awhile.

I spread out on my bunk in the single story barrack looking up at the plain wooden ceiling and crossbeams. There's nothing else to do. Our so-called classes are a joke. After a ten-minute lecture about "Voice and Command" they give us an hour off. When our free time is up, they drill us for five minutes. Why even bother? Since they had called off physical training, they give us a four-hour break. We meet again, supposedly for a pilotage navigation course. That lasts only thirty minutes instead of the three hours planned. All that is scheduled is a half hour of Morse code, a mode of communication I think is archaic. That is our day. Apparently, the purpose of being here is to kill time and learn to accept boredom, not learn anything. Lack of action dulls my sense of worth, makes me more listless than ever. I think about the old adage, "The less one does, the less once wants to do."

Our regimen reminds me of those jobs I had as a teenager when there was not enough to do, the awkwardness of it. How different from our cadet training when we hardly had a moment to rest.

There are many men like me here at Selman Field just marking time, yet the war still rages even though the Allied Forces begin to get the upper hand. It's early March 1945 and the First Army in Europe has entered Cologne, Germany, and General MacArthur is returning to Corregidor in the Philippines. B-29 bombers are devastating Tokyo and Nagoya. The end of the war is at least in sight.

Some combat veterans actually want to volunteer for another tour rather than vegetate, but the Air Corps prefers to send new men into combat. The Training Command continues turning out more pilots, navigators and bombardiers, but they have no place for them. Many fully trained navigators who graduated four months ago are still here at Selman Field, as yet unneeded. What a waste of manpower!

The weather breaks enough for physical training (PT). The ground is still soggy and treacherous from recent rains, but we exercise for nearly an hour. I imagine my idleness as shunting my blood into stagnant pools that fester in my veins. Just inhaling the air outside, breathing deeply and stretching our muscles is exhilarating. Calisthenics followed by a hot shower revives my spirit.

One program provided by the field to break the tedium and strengthen morale is offering men flights to their hometowns for the weekend, using the AT-7 training planes here at the field. The distance limit is 1500 miles. Some of the men plan to fly to New York, Chicago, Houston, even Los Angeles. I'm excited about the opportunity and will definitely take one. Even though I recently flew home on the Navy Avengers, I'm ready to go again.

Then, as it often happens in the military service, the whole program is abruptly cancelled.

At least we have the movies here on the base to entertain us. We love watching Abbott and Costello in a film about coeds. Costello dresses as a girl and plays on the women's basketball team, a scene that fills the theater with laughter. We see "Thunderhead, Son of Flicka" with Roddy McDowell and "The Scarlet Pimpernel" with Merle Oberon and Leslie Howard. "Objective Burma" with Errol Flynn is actually a decent war movie, not propaganda or impossible like so many of them. But the best films are "A Tree Grows in Brooklyn" with Dorothy McGuire and Joan Blondell even though it was sad and "A Song to Remember" about Chopin starring Cornell Wilde as Chopin and Merle Oberon as George Sand. Everyone enjoyed the last film, especially Chopin's music.

In my ample idle moments my thoughts turn to home, my friends and my parents. Every time I'm away I yearn to be back. Some of the guys don't feel that way. I suppose their home life is not as satisfying as mine. A few men have told me that they've found a home in the army.

My parents' twentieth wedding anniversary, February 28th, was just a few days ago, and I'm sorry I didn't at least send them a card. I think about the photograph of them on their wedding day, the one that is in the album at home---my father wearing a dark suit and tie, his ample black hair combed straight back, a serious expression on his face---my mother in her lacy white gown, her eyes straight ahead, a sweet smile on her lips, narrow bands of flowers around her head.

I thought about your wedding anniversary on the 28th, but when I wrote, it slipped my mind. I hope you will forgive me. I appreciate what you said about Charline and me being your biggest accomplishments, but we think the biggest thing is that our mother and father provided us with a happy home to live and grow up in. It's not the house but the loving happiness and understanding that you both put into it. I thank God that we have parents like you and realize more than ever now the value of it all. I've always said that if I could provide for my family a home as supreme as the one I grew up in, my life would be complete…More than knowledge, wealth or anything else in this world, I want that.

The Patch

═══════════════

Sitting in the co-pilot's seat of an AT-7 navigation trainer, I attempt to fly the plane, the pilot being kind or foolish enough to let me have a go at it. I'm working at maintaining altitude and flying a straight course, keeping my eye on the altimeter and compass. We're on a navigation mission to Corsicana, Texas near Dallas. The only reason I'm flying is to accumulate enough hours in the air to qualify for flight pay at the end of the month. We have three student navigators with us that are trying to reach their assigned destination, but they often drift off course and ask for new headings. As a precaution I have a map nearby folded over to show our route so I can check landmarks on the ground.

I pull back on the yoke then relax it to maintain a steady altitude, the roar and vibrations of the plane's two engines enveloping us. I'd tried the same procedure in B-17s when I flew with Johnston, but constantly overcorrected, first flying above the assigned altitude then below it, rarely at it. It's much easier in the AT-7. The air is smooth and the sky brilliant blue, the flying effortless and uneventful. For a change I'm enjoying myself. But on the way back to Selman Field we encounter clear air turbulence, our plane bouncing and bucking in the wild currents. I happily return the controls to the pilot.

A week later I fly another navigation mission, this one in a drafty AT-11. Our route is a loop to Little Rock to Fort Smith to Texarkana then back to Selman Field, icy air seeping in from the bomb bays, chilling my feet to the bone.

The weather is so erratic at Selman Field that it's constantly catching us unawares. Several times after we'd rolled out of our sacks early in the morning to report to the flight line, dark clouds sag low over the field, preventing us from flying. Then, soon after we return to the barracks, the overcast suddenly burns off. One night the stars were twinkling when we entered the movie theater, but when we came out a surprise shower drenched us. We ran through the downpour and splashed through the puddles, soaking our uniforms.

It's a rainy Saturday afternoon with nothing to do. It rained very hard a good deal of last night and most of today. It doesn't look like it's going to clear up either. It rained so hard around noon that we couldn't get to the mess hall. There was practically a river between our barracks and the mess hall. Yesterday was clear and balmy, today cloudy and wet.

Flying again makes me think about our bomber crew at Polebrook. We were so close to each other then, now we're scattered all over the country. I receive a letter from

Lucas, our flight engineer who's taking a refresher course in engineering at Amarillo, Texas. Witherspoon, our radio man, is at Reno, Nevada taking further training in radio. When he's finished, he'll join the Air Transport Command and could be sent to any part of the world. He's never liked flying but decides to stick it out. He'll train in C-46 cargo planes.

I'm sorry I don't hear further from Podoske, our co-pilot, as he was a good friend. I receive another letter from Johnston, our pilot. He had been at Laredo, Texas hauling gunners around in B-17s, but now he's at Valdosta, Georgia flying B-25s, a hot twin engine plane that lands at 130 miles per hour. He loves the plane and hopes to be a B-25 instructor. Johnston is such a skilled pilot that he'll be a superior teacher.

The commander at Selman Field orders that all of us who wear the arm patches of our former units must remove them and replace them with the standard Air Corps patch. I wear my 8th Air Force patch proudly and consider it a mark of distinction, so taking it off is a blow to my pride. I comply because I must, but the winged "8" is part of my identity. I reluctantly cut the threads binding it to my uniform then with clumsy fingers sew on the new one. At Midland we were forbidden to wear our A-2 leather jackets, many of the combat veterans having decorated them with the symbols of their group, now they take away our patch. Do they think we feel superior to the other men? Are they commanders who have never been overseas? Are they jealous of the veterans? Is it a way of "shaping us up?" What is it? The 8th Air Force patch is a symbol of all that I have been through---all of those bombing missions, the tension and memories of that time---and now I must give it up, loosen those threads and file the patch away with my mementos.

A squadron of B-17s roars high over Selman Field, undoubtedly from nearby Alexandria where I trained with my crew many months before. In one way I feel for the men in those bombers, knowing that they are in the final phase of training before going overseas. Their formation is tight and precise so they must be near the end of their crew training. They are about to face what I left behind. Each one of them must feel the apprehensions of what lies ahead. On the other hand I envy them because they are at least doing something ---bonding with each other and flying with real purpose.

Soon they'll be wearing new patches on their shoulders, either that of the 8th Air Force in England or the 15th Air Force in Italy. I have just stripped mine off; they are about to sew theirs on.

A Bottle of Beer

───────

A WAAC officer is in charge of our mess hall here at Selman Field. All our meals are tasty, I think, because of a woman's touch. I suppose I relate it to my mother's cooking, but every dish served here is a degree better than that served when a man is in charge. Our food in the officer's mess costs us $42.50 per month, taking a large bite out of our paychecks, but the food is so good we don't complain.

On my first Saturday at the mess hall I'm surprised to see cold bottles of beer lined up in boxes at the head of the chow line. Beer was never offered at any other bases. I had never had a bottle of beer before, abstaining from alcohol all of my life in response to my family that never drank, the church that frowned on all drinking and especially my high school track coach who warned us of its dangers. I look at the dark green bottles, grab one by its moist neck and place it on my tray. I hardly know what I'm doing, but the beer is free and there---and well, if I don't like it, I can always dump it out. Perhaps it's boredom, my sense of not caring or my indefinite future that temper my inhibitions.

At the table I lift the bottle to my lips and sip. The brew's cold, tangy, and bubbly, with a bitter aftertaste, but it's more pleasant than I expected. Each swallow tastes better than the one before.

I like its smell, a sour, musty scent that reminds me of collecting bottle caps as a kid. I used to hunt them everywhere, but mainly by large Coca Cola coolers filled with bottles of pop standing in slushy ice water. Caps pried off by the customers fell into a metal container at its side, providing a treasure. I reached in and pulled out handfuls of the metal caps. I especially sought them behind bars where I rummaged through trash for them, sometimes cutting my fingers on broken glass. I accumulated a large cardboard box of them, the beer caps with their cork liners smelling like the brew I'm drinking now.

I finish the bottle of beer, not with a feeling of guilt or of violating my moral principals, but with a sense of discovery. I finally taste what my fellow Air Force men drink by the gallons. It somehow brings me closer to those men, erases that separation from them that I had always felt.

I'm in a strange mood from weeks of waiting, a host of unknowns, doubts in my personal life. One of the men in our barracks who seems to see right through me, like glass, says to me one day,

"Hey, why are you doing this, going into radar training? You know it leads to combat again. What's the matter? Did some girl do you wrong?"

"No," I shot back, as I realized he was probably right.

I suppose I just don't care anymore. I don't want to go back into combat, but I don't want to be an instructor either. And I don't want to vegetate. I don't know what I want. It is as though my life is on hold, and I don't know what to do with it.

Every Saturday I have a bottle of beer, enjoying each one better than the last. I regret not having that drink with Podoske, our co-pilot, in the officer's club at Gander, Newfoundland on our last day before going overseas. I regret not having a beer with him in that pub in Oundle after our bicycle ride among the green hills of England. After returning from every bombing mission, shot glasses of amber Scotch whisky waited for us, all lined up on trays, offered as something to calm our nerves. The rest of my crew eagerly raised their glasses, tilted them back, and quickly drained them. I refused mine, giving it instead to Podoske, because I didn't drink. Now I regret that I didn't take mine and quaff it off like the others.

What was I afraid of? Other than the fact that "I didn't drink," what held me back? Was it because I thought it was immoral? Did I think it would injure my health? Did I think it would lead to drunkenness, addiction? Was I afraid of disappointing those I loved? Were there warning voices imprinted in my brain? Was I simply being morally stubborn?

I remember drinking a small bottle of cider in London, believing it was apple juice like we had back home. It was clear in the bottle unlike the amber color I'd known before. I simply thought the English made theirs a little different. It turned out to be hard cider with an alcoholic kick. I drank most of it before I realized its potency, my face becoming flushed, my head swimming. The others laughed at me. I felt then I had done something wrong, had gone against my own principles.

But I don't feel that way now.

The Lure of the Church

═══════════

I'm not pious, but I still cling to the notion that there is a God and that He protects people, including me. I muttered portions of the 23rd Psalm behind my oxygen mask and prayed for my safety on my bombing raids, and got through them all. That's significant to me. At the same time, I'm sure that many men voiced prayers, but were shot down anyway. The moral and the immoral, the good and the bad seemed to be blasted out of the sky equally. I ponder this. Am I egotistical to think that He picked me out to protect? Was there anything about me worthy of preserving? Am I more special than others? I don't think so. Survival on the bombing missions often seemed to be a matter of luck, blind chance, much like a game of roulette, the spin of the wheel, the clattering of the little ball. The two ideas bounce around in my head. Was it providence or the skittering roll of the dice that got me through?

Despite this nagging question I'm still drawn to the church. Being with people of like mind, singing hymns I had sung in church at home, listening to pastors delivering sermons from high pulpits, as well as the stirring, all-engrossing chords of the organ, nourish me. Perhaps it's a way of touching home without being there.

Soon after arriving at Selman Field I ride a bus into Monroe to attend a service at the Stone Avenue Methodist Church. My first experience there was so satisfying that I plan to attend the evening service too.

The evening service is a community sing followed by a sermon. I enjoy the pastor's molasses-thick, slow southern accent and his humor, but his sermon has nothing in it for me, his liquid words dripping off me like shower water.

At the service I filled out a welcome card. Having my home address, the church sent a letter to my parents that they sent back to me.

"It affords me much pleasure to state to you that your loved one was with us in worship recently. We appreciate having in our worship services those who have entered the service of our country.

We are endeavoring to be a help, a blessing to those who come our way. We wish to be a light house along the way of life, and if possible make the burden lighter for all. It is our desire to 'Live by the Side of the Road, and Be a Friend to Man'."

Included with the letter is a prayer printed on blue paper. It begins:

> In the silence of my chamber,
> I may with my savior share
> All my worries and my troubles
> As I talk with Him in prayer.

Army chaplains preach and offer advice in our base chapels, but I like going into town to civilian churches. It's like going back to the life I used to know. The following Sunday I ride into town to the Methodist Church that I attended before. As I'm very early I stroll around town. I discover another Methodist Church, this one much smaller than the one on Stone Avenue. It has white clapboard siding and a little belfry with a real bell in it. It intrigues me because of its plain, old-fashioned appearance. Curious, I walk into the sanctuary and sit in a pew near the back. Several people gaze at me, a startled look in their eyes, as though they haven't seen many servicemen here. The pew creaks, and the church smells like old linoleum, the way our library in Inglewood used to smell. Like the architecture and the décor, the service is too archaic to be meaningful to me. The pastor doesn't touch my life or alleviate my apprehensions, but it's nice to be in a place where real people wear suits and ties or colorful dresses instead of dull uniforms.

* * *

The long wait at Selman Field is finally over. I have my orders to report to Langley Field and leave by train at 1940 hours. I'm to take the Illinois Central from Monroe to Meridian, Mississippi. From Meridian I travel to Richmond, Virginia on the Southern Railroad via Atlanta, Georgia. The last leg, on the Chesapeake and Ohio, will be from Richmond to Hampton, Virginia, the location of the field.

At last I'm doing something! I'm excited about the

train trip ahead and the next stage in my military life. It's like breathing again.

After a day of stifling, humid heat, the sky erupts into a parade of thunderstorms, Monroe's send-off for my departure to Langley Field. Lightning stabs the base with a vengeance, thunder shaking the barracks. Each bolt and cannon-like blast makes me jump a mile. I guess I'm not over it yet. It's too much like flak, never knowing where or when it would burst, how close it would be.

But I don't care what my send off is like. I'm glad to be on the move again.

A Beginning at Langley Field

Being assigned an upper berth in a Pullman car is not what I want, but that's all that's left by the time the train pulls into the Monroe station. Before the porter makes up the berths I sit and gaze out of the rain-streaked window at the damp, cloud-shrouded fields and towns. I like rain, but the skies are gloomy, matching my apprehensions. I won't know anyone at the new base, and the facilities will be a mystery to me. When the berth is ready, I climb into it and drop off to sleep.

After a good night's rest, I sit by the window watching Georgia roll by. Later in the day when the train arrives in Atlanta, I have only ten minutes to catch the next one. I dash through the station with my bag, weaving my way through detraining passengers, finally jumping on the train going to Danville, Virginia. I'm in a chair car this time, but I'm comfortable enough. The skies are still gray, rain showers occasionally dappling the windows. The scenes we pass are all new to me as I had never been in this part of the country. With my habit of looking at all the towns and ever-changing landscape, I'm quite content.

The train hurtles through the night. I slump in the chair car, sleepier by the hour with no berth to bed down in. We won't arrive in Danville until 0100 hours.

At the soggy Danville station I wait in the restaurant, my train to Richmond, Virginia not due for another two and a half hours. Having a sour stomach from lack of sleep, I don't feel like eating. Instead, I chat with the man and woman who operate the twenty-four hour café. I watch them wipe the counters and polish the urns, the pungent smell of coffee heavy in the air.

At last the train to Richmond arrives, rain streaking down in front of the locomotive's yellow headlight, steam billowing from its stack. Exhausted, I board the chair car, finding that it's not crowded. I can have a whole seat to myself. I curl up in an empty one and am soon asleep, snoozing all the way to Langley Field. As soon as I arrive the clouds roll off to the east, the sun flooding the green countryside. Perhaps it's a good omen.

Langley Field perplexes me at first. The main portion of the base is a campus-like complex of permanent two-story brick buildings with tall chimneys surrounded by lawns and stately trees. These structures I learn right away are for the permanent officers. My quarters are located far away on another portion of the field at a section called Shellbank. The ground here consists of small shell fragments as if the whole area were dredged up from the bay. My shoes crunch the shells as I walk toward my barrack. Shellbank is so isolated that the mess hall is nearly a mile away.

I'm the only combat bombardier in my barrack, the other men being commissioned navigators and bombardiers that graduated only a month before. Most of them are flight officers, a grade below second lieutenant. Even though I'm only twenty, they all seem so young to me, younger than the men I trained with when I was a cadet. They act like high school kids, but I hope they'll settle down after a while.

Overseas, then at Midland and Selman Field, I was with officers who were veterans. I suppose there is a seriousness and sadness about us. That experience changed us all. Perhaps that's why the new officers in my barrack seem to act so young. Some of them walk around saying "hubba hubba" when they talk about girls, the way they've seen officers in the movies say it. There's a darkness about us veterans. We have pictures in our heads that they don't. I'll understand the new officers once I get to know them.

Only three cities of any size are near Langley Field--- Norfolk, Newport News and Richmond. I haven't been off the base yet, but I'd especially like to explore Norfolk.

The first trip off the base is an unexpected one to William and Mary College at Williamsburg. A group at the college is sponsoring a dance and invites officers from Langley to attend. Our base furnishes an army bus and driver. With twenty five other officers I head for the dance. Williamsburg is only about forty miles away, but it will take us an hour to get there. After riding all that way and anticipating an exciting evening, we discover that there are only nine girls at the dance, a great disappointment.

Three of us decide to slip out of the dance and rap on the door of one of the sorority houses. We didn't come all this way for nothing. A pretty brunette coed opens the door. We explain our problem about the dance and ask if we can visit them. Other girls hustle to the door, a bouquet of faces filling the doorway. They graciously invite us in. The lobby is just like a grand home with overstuffed chairs, settees and even a piano. After being around men for such a long time we find the young women refreshing. Talking to them, listening to their feminine voices, inhaling the subtle fragrance of them is just what we need. I sit on the piano bench with the dark-haired girl who answered the door. As she plays the piano we all sing. I think she likes me. As we leave they promise to send us formal invitations to their sorority dance on April 13th.

After leaving the girls we wander through historic Williamsburg admiring the fine old buildings with their polished brass doorknobs. The town is immaculate, *not a speck of dirt anywhere.* I plan to return and learn more about it. Just past midnight the bus leaves for the base, all of us tired and ready to doze on the way home. Red Skelton, now in the army, was in town, and some of our guys were excited about seeing him. A group of soldiers followed him around, but apparently he didn't mind.

Several days later I make good on my promise to explore Norfolk, two other men going with me. Even though it's twenty five miles from Langley Field, the trip takes us over three hours. At the main gate we catch a bus for Hampton. From here to Phoebus we ride a streetcar that reminds me of the Toonerville Trolley from the comic strips. I can picture it leaping off the tracks. I think at times we are about to do the same. How it stays on the rails is a mystery. The young woman operating the street car has to cut off the power when it is about to careen from the rails, allowing it to settle down. A bus and ferry take us to Old Point Comfort and then on to Willoughby. The last lap is a ten mile trolley ride to Norfolk.

Norfolk is jammed with sailors. When we look down the main street those thousands of sailors' caps form a bobbing sea of white. We are the only Air Corps officers in town, standing out in that white blizzard like the traditional "sore thumb." After a good dinner and a movie, we hope to find a hotel room, but none are available. We start the long trek back to Langley, this time taking the Greyhound a good part of the way.

Several days later Flight Officer Menke and I bus into Hampton to buy towels. While there we stop in at a small restaurant for Chesapeake Bay fried oysters. They're delicious! The golden pile of them is hot and tasty. The only way I had eaten oysters at home was in oyster stew where they bobbed around in a milky broth. That night at the officers club we are offered whole raw oysters in a cocktail sauce. I hesitate, squinting at those slimy-looking mollusks immersed in that red bath. I finally take one, letting it slide down my throat without chewing it. I have only one. Menke won't even try.

Trees are beginning to leaf out and the shimmering snow of dogwood blossoms is a hopeful and breathtaking sight. The year is renewing, but the war goes on, and we have much work ahead of us at Langley Field.

Back in the Air

We walk out to the flight line for a familiarization tour of the radar training planes and their equipment. As we prowl around inside a B-17, I give the new bombardiers and navigators a tour, pointing out the crew positions, the cockpit, bomb bay and radio room. I especially want to take them up in the nose where I sat in my small seat during all those bombing missions. They're impressed. It's the first time I had been in a B-17 since my last mission. The smell of the plane, touching its cold aluminum skin rekindle memories I thought were dying. My throat tightens. We'll be flying soon, but at least we won't have to worry about flak or the Luftwaffe.

Much like our procedure overseas, we roll out of bed at 0300 hours, still half asleep, our eyes only slits, or as some said, "piss holes in the snow." At 0400 hours we attend briefing, have breakfast then take off at 0600 hours. I'm an observer in a B-24 on my initial flight, the first time I have been up in a Liberator. My job is to coordinate the bomb sight with the radar man and take pictures of theoretical bomb releases. I can see very little from the nose, the bombardier having only a small window for viewing. I'm used to the B-17 where the grand, full view window affords magnificent views of the land below and the clouds around us. Being in the B-24's crowded nose is like not having enough air to breathe.

We fly nearly five hours over North and South Carolina and Virginia. Most of the time we are at 14,000 feet where we need to use our oxygen masks, much like being back in combat. On our way west we fly near a cold front, cloud turrets rising several thousand feet higher than our plane. On our return to Langley Field the front lies over Norfolk, directly in the path of our approach. At 3000 feet we hurtle into the front's gray vastness, a solid wall of rain and clouds. We can barely see our wingtips. Invisible hands shake us violently. I'm standing in the waist, hanging on. A wild updraft, like a great fist, pummels us from beneath, sending me sprawling. Rain leaks in through every minute opening. The vicious weather is over quickly, but it's rough while it lasts. Once we break out of the clouds we descend normally for a smooth landing.

A few days later we rustle out of our beds on a dark morning. Low clouds shroud our field, the ceiling so low we can't fly. We'll have to wait for the sun to burn off the overcast. When the stratus deck finally begins to break up, we take off into the thick haze. I again fly as an observer in an old but airworthy B-17F still wearing its camouflage paint. I make sure that the radar operator who is supposed to be navigating doesn't get lost. Suddenly the radar breaks down and I'm completely in charge of the navigation. Even though it's a surprise, we hit all our points on time and return to Langley Field. As we begin to let down near Norfolk, either the army or the navy is taking anti-aircraft practice. Off to our right are the sinister black puffs of exploding shells I hoped I would never see again.

Our most enjoyable flight is an overnight trip to Robin's Field in Macon, Georgia. Our group flight consists of three B-24s and two B-17s. I'm the navigator on one of the B-24s. We take off at 2000 hours Sunday night, arriving at Macon near 2330 hours. They put us up in a very nice Officers Dormitory with three-quarter beds, clean sheets and towels and hot showers. It's like staying in a hotel. We clean up then walk over to the Red Cross Canteen for sandwiches.

After staying in bed until 0830 hours the following morning, we rise and head to the mess hall where we have a hearty breakfast before looking over the field. It's the largest air depot in the South with over four hundred planes being repaired, modified or scrapped. Almost all the workers, strangely enough, are civilians. After lunch we again gaze out at the field. Other than its huge cavernous hangars and rows of planes, its runways are set in deep green, velvety grass, the edges of the field dark with forests of pine. It's spacious, clean and beautiful.

During briefing for the return trip my assignment is to be the radar operator on a B-17, another surprise. I've only learned the rudiments of a radar set up until now, a familiarization with all the knobs and switches, but have never actually operated one. Although I'm tense about the responsibility, I have an instructor with me who is patient and a good teacher as well. I'm fascinated with what I see in the circular radar scope, a sharp line of light turning like a quick clock hand around the face of it, illuminating bright patches representing land and cities, and leaving dark areas indicating the sea, lakes and rivers. I'm observing the land in a dramatic new way. When we touch down back at Langley Field, I've become the only one in our class who has flown a radar mission.

Smug and proud I jump down from the plane, visions of that sweeping hand and electronic landscapes still dancing in my head.

The Colony Inn

Having found nothing of interest in Newport News, the closest city to Langley Field, some of us ride over to Hilton Village, only a few miles away. It's a collection of steep-roofed, English style houses built by the government and the ship building companies to house shipyard workers during World War I.

We walk across a lawn under grand old shade trees to the Colony Inn. It too looks English to me with its pitched roof and cupola on top. Inside are a dance floor and a band as well as a restaurant and bar. I'm not a good dancer, my only lessons years ago at the Bessie Clark School of Dancing when I was a freshman in high school. But I summon enough courage to ask a girl to dance. We slide around the floor well enough, I carefully avoiding her toes. The band plays "I'll Walk Alone", the music slow and sweet. The warm touch of her hand, the pressure of my arm around her waist, her closeness, awake tenderness within me I had not felt for months.

"I'd like to see you again some time," I say.

"Oh, that would be nice," she says.

The chance of our getting together again is remote. And we both know it.

On Saturday nights most of the men show up at the Colony Inn as it's the only action in town. This Saturday night is no exception. Several of us drop by for dinner and drinks. I'm surprised that all four of their waiters are Italian prisoners of war. They speak very little English, but through sign language and a few words I remember from my high school Latin class I carry on a limited conversation with some of them. One is from Milan, another from Turin, the other two from Rome. I chat mainly to the man from Milan, slender in his waiter's uniform, his ample hair dark and wavy, his facial features classical Italian. He had been an engineer in the Italian Army and was taken prisoner at Palermo, Sicily. He had retreated all the way from El Alamein. He tells me that Rome is the best place to go in Italy and that Naples is the worst. He says that Naples is even worse than Newport News. He hasn't seen his family in over three years. I enjoy talking to him and sympathize with his sadness. Perhaps because we are both combat veterans we feel a certain kinship with each other, even though we're on different sides.

The Colony Inn is like a fancy Officers Club since there are so many officers there on Saturday night. It's where I was introduced to Coke Highs, Coca Cola mixed with a shot of bourbon. The drink tastes like a refreshing glass of

Coca Cola, but the effects are startlingly different. As I sip them I begin to feel a sense of well being, a melting away of inhibitions, a release. I find it easier to talk to people, to be bolder in expressing myself in conversations. I discover the great secret of why people drink.

One drink is very pleasant, but two is even better. Sometimes I lose track of how many I've downed. As I walk back to the barracks with several others, I'm aware that I'm talking louder than usual, sometimes yelling. It's as though I'm outside of myself looking down at this obnoxious person, wondering who he is. Shouts escape out of me like phantoms I can't control. The others look at me and laugh. Have I become one of those rowdy, whiskey-reeking soldiers that tumble clumsily into the barracks at night, disturbing all the sleepers? The ones who have broken into my sleep so many times?

I don't write a word to my parents about Coke Highs and how they affect me or even about the beers I had consumed at Selman Field. I know they, being teetotalers, would worry about me---and maybe they should. I know that my parents, my church friends and my revered track coach would be upset by my imbibing, but I'm not the same person as I was when I first entered the service, that completely innocent kid.

I've been back from overseas for only a few months and have never dealt with the terror of those bombing missions. I still have nightmare-like pictures in my head. I know that I'm tense and restless, at loose ends. All those experiences must be working on me, accumulating inside of me, like water behind a dam. Maybe that's why a Coke

High gives me such a sense of relief. Perhaps the reason I howl is to release the yell I should have let fly on those missions. Who knows?

Next Saturday night will again find me at the Colony Inn.

The Orderly

"Pop," our civilian barracks orderly, lies motionless on the wooden floor in his private room. He's just a little bag of bones weighing a hundred pounds, maybe less. We easily lift him onto his bed, the sharp smell of whiskey on his breath. He groans softly as we lay him on his top blanket, his breathing shallow, the white stubble on his face like a thin frost. As most of his teeth have rotted away, his ruddy cheeks are hollow. His sunken eyes are shut now in alcoholic slumber, but when he's awake he gazes at us with washed out blue eyes rimmed with red.

This isn't the first time we've picked him up like a loose sack of potatoes and deposited him in his bed. His job is to keep the barracks clean and warm and make sure our water is hot. For this service he's given a small room at the end of our barrack and a modest stipend. He spends a hefty portion of his paycheck on whiskey and, it's rumored, prostitutes in nearby Hampton. He seems to be in various stages of drunkenness most of the time. Now and then he forgets or is not sober enough to stoke up the furnace and supply us with hot water for showers. When we jump under a shower that nearly takes our breath away, we yell at him.

If it weren't for this job, he'd be living in an alley or a homeless shelter. It's a good deal for him, having a roof over his head, a paycheck and our good company.

But in his rheumy eyes there's a twinkle, a spark of life. He's a pleasant fellow as he sweeps the barracks floor, joking and chatting with the men. Even though we're angry with him sometimes, we all like him.

In his youth, he tells us, he was an exerciser of race horses and a jockey. He was also a stable sergeant during World War I and a feather weight boxer.

"Yeah, when I was a jockey we had to keep our weight down or we couldn't ride. You know how we did it! We'd bury ourselves in a pile of horse shit and hay and stay there for hours. God, it would get hot under there You'd sweat so much the pounds would melt away. You don't believe me? No shit, that's what we'd do."

But we didn't know anything about his childhood and family life, his youth and journey into manhood. We see him as an old man, a hopeless drunk, knowing little about memories that lurk in his mind.

Another officer and I knock then enter his room one day finding him sitting on his bed apparently sober. My friend pulls out a half-empty bottle of bourbon and holds it up to him. "Hey, would you like a drink?" Pop's eyes light up as he opens them wide, his tongue licking his upper lip, running slowly from one side to the other. It is as though he's transfixed, his whole being locked on the amber whiskey in that bottle. I think it's cruel teasing him like that, adding to his misery, abetting his alcoholism. My friend gives him a gulp, and we leave the room. Rumor has it that he can down a whole drinking glass of whiskey just as we drink a glass of water.

The results of Pop's negligence occur more often. On a frigid April morning the barrack is so cold it's painful to get out of bed. As we throw back the covers and shiver on the cold floor, we curse Pop who blissfully sleeps in his stupor, having allowed the furnace to die.

A few days later Gafford and I check on him, finding him on the floor again, this time huddled in one corner of his room. As usual we lift him to his bed.

Shortly afterward, due to numerous complaints, the base fires him. When he was sober he was a pleasant guy with a good sense of humor. Now he's headed for an alley or maybe the Old Soldiers Home--- and we miss him.

The Jersey Bounce

Getting there on time will take a miracle. My flight as an observer on a B-24 lasted much longer than I'd planned. How am I ever going to catch the 1400 ferry from Old Point Comfort? I strip off my flying clothes, dash in for a quick shower and jump into my dress uniform. Menke, whose home is in Roselle, New Jersey, had asked me to go home with him this weekend. His radar flight was over earlier, so he was able to board the 1100 ferry. The plan now is that he'll meet me at the Newark train station then take me to his home, but I have a long way to go.

With luck I reach the ferry on time, board the creosote-smelling steamer and sit down with a sigh in one of its many seats. It's crowded with other passengers heading for points north, the babble of their voices filling the large cabin. We strike out across bay for a slow two-hour trip to Cape Charles, Virginia, but it's nice to relax for a while, watch the sea flow by and be lulled by the ship's gentle rocking.

At Cape Charles I step into one of the dusty red coaches of the Pennsylvania Railroad's fast trains to New York. On the train the countryside flies by, but what I see captivates me---rural scenes, farms and forests, all shades of rich green. We speed through Maryland and Delaware, stopping at Wilmington, a steel and ship-building city. As day shades into night the train passes through Philadelphia then on to Trenton and Newark. I'm relieved to see Menke and his father waiting for me on the station platform.

Many of the men in my radar class had become my good friends, but I seem to bond more with Menke. He's a gentle guy, rather boyish in looks, taller than I am and with a shock of blond hair. I welcome the opportunity to be with a family again. Menke's father is very kind and respectful to me. We drive home to Roselle where I meet his mother, a kind and considerate woman just like my own mother. It's like I'm home again.

After only fifteen minutes in their house Menke and I are off in his family car to pick up his girl friend in Linden, about five miles away. She also provides a girl for me. The four of us then arrive at a home that belongs to one of Menke's family friends who happens to not be at home. But they have loaned Menke a key. Their cellar has been converted into a large recreation room with rows of gleaming liquor bottles and an open floor large enough for dancing. Besides that they have a first class record player and stacks of records. For several hours we pour ourselves drinks and dance in the dim light. Susan, my girl, is no better at dancing than I am, but we manage, moving around the floor hanging on to each other. A plump young woman with a pretty face, she is both shy and quiet.

We take a break from dancing and drive to Surprise Lake, the water surrounded by pines, a scene I didn't think existed in New Jersey, having thought it mainly flat and fouled with industry. The air is fresh and the moon is bright, and for an hour or two we walk around in the electric-blue moonlight, talking and enjoying the atmosphere. We return to the house for more dancing until we begin to notice that it's getting light outside. After dropping the girls off at 0600 we drive back to Menke's house, getting to bed by 0730. We sleep until noon.

After a quick breakfast we walk down his street, dropping in on some of the neighbors. Everyone is very friendly, and welcomes us into their homes. I feel like I'm back on Brett Street in Inglewood basking in the warmth of friends. Being with "real" people in civilian homes is so very different from the ranks of uniformed men and the sterility of the barracks that I'm used to.

Mrs. Menke prepares a bountiful dinner of roast beef, potatoes and tasty gravy, a meal that my mother or grandmother would have had on Sundays. Menke's cousin Jean and her girlfriend drop in, both 18 and quite pretty. They decide to take me to a pond where they often ice skate in winter. It's a long walk, but the small pond bordered with trees is worth seeing, and our conversations are easy. I haven't had a good time like this in a long while, actually walking with two nice girls as though I'm a civilian. Flying, radar missions and the war suddenly seem very far away.

When we return to the house, two more young men and a girl have arrived, the living room beginning to fill up. We all gather around Menke as he plays the piano, singing together until our throats are raspy.

As the night progresses we know it's about time to leave and return to the base. At the Newark station Menke and I board a train to New York so we'll be able to get a seat on the crowded train south to Cape Charles. The train burrows under the Hudson, the pressure inside the tunnel stuffing my ears. Our train leaves Penn Station at 2300. We travel all night in a chair car, dozing off now and then, but arriving tired and heavy-eyed. We catch the ferry at 0700, arriving at the base at 0930.

It was a rush deal, but worth it in every way. I don't know when I have enjoyed myself so much. They want me to come back.

* * *

The next weekend Menke and I rush to catch the 2100 ferry on Saturday night. We don't arrive in Newark until 0630 Sunday, but Menke's dad and his sister, whom I had not met last time, are there to meet us. She is 23 and recently married, her husband a B-29 co-pilot now headed for the Pacific.

We have another very nice Sunday dinner then all of us go to the Methodist Church for a service. Afterwards I take a long walk with Menke's cousin Jean. She is nice and easy to talk to and reminds me of my sister Charline. We plan a date next week in New York.

I sleep most of the way back on the train. I'm sore when I wake up, having been slumped in an awkward position for so long. We arrive back at the base just in time for classes.

* * *

New Jersey is becoming my normal weekend destination. Even though we often fly radar missions and spend endless hours studying radar operations, bombing and navigation in ground school, my thoughts tend to wander far up north to the Garden State.

The following weekend I again miss the early ferry and am slowed down even more when the train is an hour late reaching Newark. Even though I arrive close to midnight, Menke and his girl along with Jean meet me at the station. As it's now too late to go to New York we settle on the Terrace Room in a hotel in Newark. Their band and floor show is just what we want, but they close at 0200. By the time we get to another place in Elizabeth they are playing "Goodnight Sweetheart", their last tune of the night. One swing around the dance floor, and we're finished.

The next day is clear and sunny when Jean and I catch the electric train at Linden for the short trip into New York. Menke had to return to Langley Field to fly, but the family insisted that I stay, almost as though I were one of them. Once out of Penn Station we walk about ten blocks to Times Square. The hustle of New York amazes me, everyone moving so fast, the cars and taxies honking at each other, the wail of sirens. We decide to book a walking tour, a guide taking us on the elevated railway, the subway and buses to see the sights up close. Our whirlwind tour takes us to the Trinity Church, Wall Street, the Coffee and Cotton Exchange, Chinatown, the Bowery, the Brooklyn Bridge, Radio City and Rockefeller Center as well as distant views of Ellis Island and the Statue of Liberty. I'm surprised that the elevated train takes us so close to the shabby tenement houses, sometimes roaring right past their windows. It reminds me of all the movies I had seen in which tenement families endure the shaking of their room, the grinding din and flashing windows of the trains as they thunder by.

I had returned from England by ship, the USS Excelsior, giving me my first view of the clustered skyscrapers of Manhattan and the Statue of Liberty. Upon landing they had put us on a train for Camp Kilmer in New Jersey, not allowing us to explore the city. Now much later I'm getting that chance, and every sight and sound excites me.

Exhausted from our tour, we have chow mein and egg rolls at a Chinese restaurant before we catch the train "home."

* * *

The following week Mr. and Mrs. Menke drive down to Langley Field to see the facilities for themselves and to haul us back up to New Jersey. At New Castle, Delaware we drive onto a ferry to Pennsville, New Jersey then endure a slashing rain with blue flashes of lightning all the way to Roselle.

The next evening Menke, Jean and I pick up his girlfriend then drive to Jersey City to take the ferry across the Hudson. Once in New York we duck into a Chinese restaurant for more chow mein. We decide to go to the ice show at the Center Theater called "Hats off to Ice." Sonya Heine is the director, but she's not in the show. The entire stage is covered with ice, and the graceful skaters with fantastic costumes glide across in acts that astound me. I had never seen anything like it. I sit there spellbound at the color and movement on the stage.

Afterwards we walk to the Hotel Astor where we take the elevator to the top floor for dancing. Many others have the same idea, and people are lined up to get in. Discouraged and about to leave, we meet an acquaintance of Menke's who already has a table. He invites us to join him, so we pass by the others in the line who give us unhappy looks. We gather around a table that looks like those I have seen in movies, draped with linen, a small lamp in the middle. We order drinks. Sammy Kaye leads his band, and dancers crowd the floor. Jean and I attempt to dance, but the floor is so jammed that we constantly bump into other couples. It's great to be dancing to the music of Sammy Kaye though. I have some of his records at home, and have always liked the mellow sound of his band. As we dance his music is being broadcast live over the radio. I'm in the middle of something big. My God! Dancing to Sammy Kaye and the same music I'm dancing to being broadcast over the radio!

The dancing over, now out in the fresh air again, we walk to the car. We drive along the Hudson River and over the Washington Bridge, arriving in Roselle about 0500. New York is expensive, but because we're shipping out soon, this is almost certainly our last trip north, and worth a splurge.

Menke and I sleep until noon, rest awhile then begin the trip back to reality---the base and the war. Several other men from our field are on the train back. We have a lot to talk about so I get very little sleep. A half hour after we return to the field we're immersed in navigation exams and New Jersey becomes only a dream.

Bittersweet

The war looks a little better now that American tanks patrol the streets of major German cities. They bring peace to places like Ludwigshaven when only a short time ago their flak batteries had thrown up murderous barrages that we had to fly through to bomb their chemical plants. In the skies high over that city a jagged shard of shrapnel from the barrage dug into Podoske's thigh. It's where they shot out our oxygen system forcing us to scramble for spare bottles. In a way, the taking of the city is a kind of revenge for what they did to us. Personally I feel a warm sense of satisfaction. Germany can't hold out much longer.

When we flew over Germany we watched for enemy jet fighters, planes so fast they could outrun our best fighter plane, the P-51 Mustang. Our bombers often blasted the jet aircraft assembly plants, trying to delay their production. The Germans, far advanced in jet and rocket technology, had developed their super plane, the Messerschmitt 262, and Hitler was going to win the war with them. I never saw any, but I scanned the skies for them.

At Langley Field I see my first jet plane, not German, but American.

It was a Bell Aircomet, a P-59. It didn't land, but it swooshed over the field this morning a couple of times and then this afternoon once. What a noise that thing makes. It's a combination of a roar and a swishing sound. It left just a slight trail of dark smoke behind it. It was moving very fast and was soon out of sight. If you ever hear queer noises in the sky out there, it will probably be that plane.

* * *

Well tonight is a very sad night indeed. The death of the president came as a great shock to us all. It just stunned me so. I could hardly believe it. Somehow I just couldn't help a few unnoticeable tears. He just seemed like the United States itself, something I fought for and seen boys die for. It's just a shame that he couldn't see the end of the war. I only hope our new president will do as well and that the country gets behind him.

I never knew any other president. When Hoover was in office, I was too young to care. My fiercely Republican, teetotaling grandparents, however, loved Hoover and hated Roosevelt. They wanted Hoover to win the election. "If we vote for Roosevelt, he'll bring back beer," they warned. They were all for prohibition and against the evils of drink, but I thought they were just old fashioned.

Franklin Roosevelt had done so much to pull our

country out of the depression, by starting works programs like the WPA, the CCC and the NRA. The New Deal gave people back their dignity and put food on the table.

Mr. Homburg, two doors down from my house in Inglewood, wields a shovel for the WPA. Otherwise he would be out of work. He still gleans dry lima beans in the hills after the threshers go by and raises chickens, killing one for dinner by grabbing its head and swinging it around in a circle to break its neck. Of course most of the families at home raise chickens, gather eggs and plant gardens to supplement shrinking wages.

Roosevelt was our wartime president, our leader. He was like a father that most of us looked up to. We always gathered around the radio when he gave his Fireside Chats. He had the most eloquent voice, the confidence and optimism he exuded boosting the nation's morale in difficult times. April 12, 1945 is a sad day for all of us.

* * *

German cities are falling like ten pins and rumors have it that the Nazis are fleeing to Norway. We hear that the enemy has given up, but there's nothing official, just stories. We don't know what to believe. In the midst of all the hearsay, the base commander cancels all flights and ground school for tomorrow and tells us to prepare for a gigantic parade.

Then it becomes official, VE-Day has arrived, May 8, 1945. Now there's no way that we'll be sent to Europe other than to bolster the occupation. All those flak guns that used to fill the sky with their deadly shrapnel are silenced. The Luftwaffe is grounded, most of their planes only tangled aluminum. Now Japan is our only enemy, and with the full force of our military might directed against them they're bound to capitulate.

Today we had a big parade and what an ordeal that was. First we had a practice and then the real thing. Altogether we marched about five miles around Langley Field. Many turned out to watch us. We were all dressed up in our suntans...Well anyway we are all pretty tired from walking. Quite a few "bit the dust" when we had to stand out there on the ramp and listen to long addresses. The ambulances were busy picking everybody up. The WAACs were hitting the ground today too.

If Roosevelt had lived another month and a week he would have seen the end of the war in Europe. All of us are heartened that the war is winding down, that most of us are going to live and return to our homes to begin our lives-- to become what we are to be. . .

Getting to Know the Men

Tired of vegetating, we find it a great relief to be starting our first radar ground school classes. At Midland and Selman Field the base commanders didn't know what to do with the returning veterans from overseas. As a consequence we accomplished very little other than reviewing what we already knew in makeshift classes and getting in our flying time.

At least now I have some direction--- to become a radar observer. My compass needle is aligned on a definite course instead of flipping randomly in all directions.

Because I'm a first lieutenant, the officers in charge make me a unit leader responsible for fifteen men. I have to see that they get to classes on time and study their lessons. I don't relish being responsible for anyone, but I have no choice.

Our ground school hours are long, usually beginning at 0800 and sometimes ending at 1930. Our classes cover electronics, electricity, radar theory, radio and the operation of the radar set. I like working with the Buck Rogers stuff and maintain a high grade average. The courses are difficult, the instructors throwing figures and diagrams at us without mercy. Some of the teachers bore us with their monotone voices or irk us with their know-it-all cockiness, but we do our best to learn from them. Examinations are given every day and will lead to a four-hour final exam at the end of the course.

Morale is poor at the base, its contagion affecting us all. The permanent officers, the ones that live in the fine brick buildings surrounded by park-like grass and trees, are competing with each other, and are locked in a political battle. At most bases the programs are built around flying, but here the ground school and its personnel are dominant. As a result we fly at odd hours, while those for the ground school remain steady. For example, returning from a long flight, tired and hungry, we find that the mess hall is closed. No provision is made for us, the personnel operating only at times convenient for them. We're forced to settle for salami sandwiches at the PX.

During the final exam with the room silent and everyone's mind locked on the test, a carpenter begins sawing next door, the sound a penetrating buzzing and screeching. It's as though he saws through our brains, everyone stopping, their concentration shattered. The carpenter gets the word and the test continues.

* * *

Being the unit leader gives me an opportunity to observe the men, know them better.

After I'm better acquainted with the men in the barracks, I find I like most of them. At first they seemed immature to me, like high school students with their joking and their lack of seriousness. Time shapes them into likeable, considerate men that I'm happy to be with. Most are like me, only in the military because of necessity, wanting the war to be over, and biding their time until they can begin their real lives.

They are all second lieutenants and flight officers, so I and one other first lieutenant outrank them. They look up to me because of my rank, but mostly because I'm a combat veteran. Being admired is a new experience for me. Among the many men returning from overseas at Midland and Selman Field, I was just another veteran.

One of the second lieutenants, a red head, stops me outside the barracks door. He looks straight into my eyes then drops his gaze as he points to the ribbons on my tunic. "I'd give almost anything to have the medals you've earned, but I wouldn't want to do what you had to do to get them."

Although I bond with most of the men, I'm vastly different from others. One man in particular, Winslow, somewhat older than the rest, and generally aloof from the group goes out on his dates alone. Leaving for his dates, he walks ramrod-straight down the middle of the barracks, looking only ahead, his shoes pounding out a purposeful rhythm on the wooden floor, a superior smirk on his face. Those who know him say he always has two women lined up when he leaves, one for early in the evening and one for later. They are not soda parlor dates, but heavy encounters involving his apparently unlimited sexual stamina.

While most of us look forward to leaving the military as soon as possible, a few have found a niche in the Army Air Corps. One of them is Stucky. He says, "I haven't got anything or anybody outside the army. I like it here. It's like home to me." One reason he likes it is that there are plenty of women that buzz around the airfield like libidinous hornets. I hear them with him sometimes outside of the barracks with their harsh voices, their coarseness and silliness. One of girls is irked at Stucky and tells a friend to "tell Stucky that he can take a flying f--- at a rolling donut."

A few other men like these girls, their looseness and street toughness appealing to them. One of them, Kaiser, plump for a military man, his face innocent and boyish, hangs around with Stucky and the girls. The others tell me the girls can't keep their hands off him, and he loves it. I recognize his voice coming from the girls' car as they drive up to the Shellbank barracks, their raucous laughter and giggles rising out of the car windows like coarse bubbles in cheap champagne.

Stucky is a comical guy and despite our differences I like him and often laugh at his antics. We have a single phone on the wall in the barracks, the man closest to it answering it when it rings. Stucky picks up the ringing phone as he passes by. Talking in a serious voice he says, "Stucky Carpet Service. We lay anything."

The slutty women repel me. They're loud, crude and vulgar, not like the girls at home or the ones I met in New Jersey, Menke's friends.

The men, with all their differences, all sleep in the same barracks, eat together, fly with each other and take the same classes in ground school. We all tolerate one another. It is to our advantage to get along, and we do.

Men of the Past

―――――――

I often think about my combat crew and sometimes receive letters from them. Having trained at different bases scattered across the country, we had all come together at Alexandria Army Airfield in Louisiana. Training there for twelve weeks, we gradually became an efficient crew ready to go overseas. We flew a bomber across the Atlantic to England then remained together during most of our thirty-four stressful bombing missions, each of us enduring them in our own way.

When we returned to the states from Europe, we were all dispersed to different parts of the country, and I miss those men. When our crew left England, Podoske, our co-pilot and my best friend, as well as Caruso, our ball turret gunner, were still in the hospital recovering from shrapnel wounds.

Johnston, always the consummate pilot and able commander, is now taking an instrument course at Bryan, Texas where he flies single engine AT-6 training planes.

Being used to four engine bombers that respond slowly, he finds himself overcorrecting the smaller planes. He hopes to return to Georgia where he'll fly larger planes again.

Lucas, our flight engineer, is at Chanute Field, Illinois taking a course in technical instruments. I always felt he didn't have much use for me, didn't like taking any orders from a nineteen-year-old kid who was an officer, yet he writes me as a friend. He tells me that Stanowick, our tail gunner, now at Truax Field in Wisconsin, has been grounded for three months with combat fatigue. We were all fatigued, but perhaps him more than any of us.

Lucas reports that the officers are so strict at Chanute Field that he and most of the other enlisted men are burning mad. He thinks it's a plot by the officers to make them volunteer for another tour of combat duty just to get away from them. At least Lucas is close enough to his hometown in Michigan that he can get there on weekends. I wish I were that close to my hometown.

I find out that Witherspoon, our radio man, is overseas again, not in England as before, but in Karachi, India. He flies with the ATC, the Air Transport Command. From his base in Karachi he can fly anywhere in the world. The irony is that he was the one man on our crew who never wanted to fly again. He had trouble with air sickness during our training, and was, according to the other crew members, very pale after each of our missions. I feel so sorry for him that I ask my mother to send him a batch of homemade cookies, perhaps her special icebox cookies.

Later, Witherspoon writes me a letter. He says he was bitter at first when the ATC sent him overseas again, but that he has calmed down now. As compensation for being sent to India he has clean sheets on his bed, twenty four-hour laundry service and showers with warm water. He's also making a lot of money as the ATC pays per diem when he's away from his base.

Sometimes I hear about friends I had made in training. One good friend was Johnny Sacks. I had heard a rumor before that he had been shot down, but now a letter from a friend confirms it.

I had some pretty bad news today. One of my very best friends was killed in Europe. He was a radar operator on a B-17. His name was Johnny Sacks. He slept in the bed next to me at Ellington Field, and we became pretty close friends. When we had our overnight pass there, he and I got our hotel room together, went to church together and everything. We both went to Laredo for gunnery. When I got sick at Laredo, he went on to the bombardier school at San Angelo. I went to Midland a week later. I never saw him again until a place called Stone, England. We were both so surprised to see each other, and we talked over old times for two days. That was the last I saw of him and ever will. He was really a fine, upstanding fellow and very close to his family. I know how they must feel.

I learn too that a plane from our field returning to the United States crashed into a hillside in stormy weather while attempting to land at Valley, Wales. Among those killed in the crash was Howard Hibbard, the pilot who had once nursed his badly damaged plane back to England. We had picked him up as well as his co-pilot and navigator at an emergency field close to the English Channel. He became our co-pilot after Podoske was hurt. The dead also included Santo Caruso our ball turret gunner who was so badly wounded on our third mission, spending months recovering in the hospital. Our base meteorological officer, our weather man, who always played the little GI organ at our chapel services, was also among the dead. They were all great guys who thought they were on their way home---instead they perished among the twisted aluminum scattered over that misty hill that they did not see.

Now and then I happen on some friend from the past. One of them is a navigator from our bomb group in England, Carlton Mendell, a member of Hibbard's crew. He was passing through when I came across him in one of our hangars. His crew, Hibbard's, slept right across from us in our barracks at Polebrook. One day, when his plane was riddled and ripped by flak, they tried to make it back to England alone. Since they had to fly low, they were a good target for ground fire. Hibbard, the pilot, thinking they might not make it back, ordered his crew to bail out over Germany. Mendell was at the hatch ready to jump when he noticed that the pilot and co-pilot were making no moves to abandon the plane. When he asked them what they were going to do, the co-pilot said they had decided to try and reach England, asking Mendell for a heading. By a combination of luck and skill the three of them crossed the English Channel and reached an airfield on the coast.

Our crew flew to this landing strip to pick them up. Their plane, having made it on two engines, was ripped and torn by shells, shrapnel and bullets. I was amazed that it could still fly. The three remaining members of the crew, including Mendell, were pale and badly shaken. The men who had bailed out were all captured and made prisoners of war.

I'm dumbfounded to see Mendell in the hangar at Langley Field. He tells me that about two days after we left he was on a mission to Politz, Germany with another crew when their plane was pummeled with flak and badly damaged. Seeing no way they could make it back to England, they flew to Sweden, still neutral in the war. They flew low over the Baltic, zigging and zagging as they were chased by two Focke Wulf 190s. He was held in Sweden for two months before their government gave them permission to leave.

They left in a B-24 that would have to take a chance flying over occupied Norway to get back to England. They flew purposely in stormy weather to avoid German interceptors.

Mendell tells me that another plane from our field attempted to land at the same field in Sweden, but hit a granite knoll and crashed, killing all but two of the crew. He also says that 144 planes were sent to Politz that day and 44 of them were shot down. Apparently the Germans, tipped off about the target, had amassed anti-aircraft guns and deployed extra interceptor planes to protect it.

I can't help but think that if I had stayed at Polebrook only a few more days, I would have been on that mission. Such is the roulette wheel of luck, the one that spun every time we took off. Where, we wondered, would the little ball land?

Radar Man

═══════════════

I'm an observer on a B-17 flying an assigned pattern to Philadelphia, Reading, Wilmington, New York City, Newark and Trenton and back to Langley Field. As I'm in the bombardier's position with its large Plexiglas window and the weather is sparkling clear, I have a great view of the Statue of Liberty when we reach New York. It's the first time I've seen the great lady well since our ship from Liverpool entered New York Harbor months ago, returning us from duty with the 8th Air Force in England. I remember what a glorious day that was. I can see the Empire State Building among the skyscrapers of Manhattan, and farther away, Coney Island.

On the way back we fly through two growing thunderheads. We enter them at 10,000 feet, riding the turbulence like a ship on a stormy sea. Updrafts kick us hundreds of feet higher. Downdrafts drop us as though we're in a plunging elevator, with the same feeling in the pit of my stomach. The plane creaks like an un-oiled door and the wings are flapping. I hang on tight in the nose compartment.

Our buffeting is not quite as severe as that encountered by a friend of mine. Flying in the weather ship, he had flown into a large thunderhead at 32,000 feet. When they broke out of the clouds, being beaten by the wild currents, other cloud turrets still rose far above them. When this same weather system drifted over Langley Field where I was, it dumped torrents of rain with violent lightning and thunder.

We continue rising in the wee hours of the morning, keeping most of us in a state of perpetual exhaustion. Since I have had a radar flight and the rest of the class has had none, I again fly as a navigator-observer. As often happens, the radar fails to function properly, and I'm left to do all the navigation to the selected cities and back to the base again. I'm dead tired and heavy-eyed, but guiding the plane with my headings gives me a lot of satisfaction.

Either fog or storminess often prevents or delays our flying. One night as we are second in line for take off, a thick fog suddenly rolls in off the bay. Our flight being cancelled, we taxi back to the flight line. Several planes had already taken off, one taking a chance on landing in the mist, the others flying off to Richmond for the night.

The following day I fly as the radar operator on a B-24. I'm again mesmerized by what I see on the scope, the bright splotches of land, the even brighter cities, the darkness of rivers and bays. Heavy rainstorms, especially thunderstorms send back bright echoes that look like cities. More than one flight has flown into storms thinking they were cities. I'm so busy operating the radar, plotting our headings and lining up targets on this four- hour flight that the time passes quickly. I like my little niche on the plane, a small metal table in front of me, the set with its scope and adjustment knobs, my altimeter and air speed indicator, the muscular bundles of wires. It's like my cozy cubbyhole.

Radar is not perfected yet. As soon as we take off the following day on a radar mission I discover that my set is not functioning. We return to the field and pick up a radar mechanic who can't make it work either. We have to scrub the mission. I remember overseas that the radar observers were always having problems, the sets operating like cantankerous old men, sometimes reasonable, sometimes cranky and nasty.

My rating has changed from Aerial Observer (Bombardier) to Aerial Observer (Radar). I fly again later as a radar operator, the radar set working properly. I have no problems and feel I've finally mastered the equipment. I'm confident I can interpret the land I fly over and can guide a plane to any target. The problem on this flight is the refrigerator- cold conditions in the airplane, my hands red and stiff, making it difficult to adjust the dials and knobs. We fly though miles of high clouds, the minute ice crystals that compose them filtering in through every tiny opening like frozen dust.

On another day we take off just twenty minutes before a cold front hits Langley Field. It's my first of two radar check rides. We fly at 21,000 feet, skirting cloud turrets rising even higher than our altitude. The rain along the cold front as well as several isolated thunderstorms show clearly on my radar scope, so I can guide the plane around them. The flight goes well. We have no problems dodging the foul weather, and the instructor approves of my radar skills.

A few days later I fly as an observer, my mind foggy from lack of sleep and our heavy schedule. We cruise at 10,000 feet, winding our way through a fantastic forest of towering clouds, unstable air bubbling with convection currents. Where there are strong local updrafts the clouds pile into pillars or narrow columns. In all my hundreds of hours in the air, I have never seen anything like it. I'm still fascinated with flying, not only to behold grand vistas of the earth below but also to sail among the clouds, a magical place that non-flyers know nothing about.

We must be wary of thunderstorms at this time of year. One of our B-17s flew directly into a mature thunderstorm, the radar operator again thinking it was a city. Wild currents caught them, throwing them into a spin. The pilot regained control at 4,000 feet, but the co-pilot and the flight engineer had already bailed out, thinking the situation hopeless. The co-pilot is okay, but they haven't found the engineer yet.

We never know what to expect. One of my friends had to bail out of a B-17 when an engine caught fire. He floated down to a field in North Carolina. A curious crowd of country folk gathered around him, amazed to see a flyer drop out of the sky. Not knowing what to do, they just stood there looking at him, some apparently thinking he was from outer space. Finally one man got up enough nerve to ask him where he was from.

Flying continues at a fast pace. I've logged sixteen hours in the last four days. A night time flight north of Langley Field gives me my first glimpse of our National Capitol Building, its dome illuminated with flood lights. Although we fly at 10,000 feet and the dome looks small from our altitude, it's wonderful to see. Gazing down on it gives me a sense of pride. We cruise back over Baltimore with its shipyards beneath us, its bright lights aglow, the flickering arcs of welding torches as bright as stars.

I'm forever astounded by the sights I witness from the air. On one mission we break through the cloud tops at 5,000 feet then fly higher over them. At 14,000 feet, the cloud deck below is a vast moonlit plain, a dazzling sea of lunar blue with a tapestry of stars above. I'm reminded again how in love I am with flying.

My last flight is my final check flight as an APS-15 radar operator. Even though I'm naturally tense, everything goes well, and my instructor is satisfied. I've also finished the radar ground trainers, so I have little left to do. I now have sixty hours in B-24s and twenty in B-17s here at Langley.

That should wrap up my training at Langley Field.

Heading West

The hard boiled eggs at the Officers Club, piles of them in every color of the rainbow, are not enough to get me into the Easter spirit. Within the slow ache of my home sickness I think about my family's Easter dinner--- slices of ham and steaming scalloped potatoes, especially the pickled eggs my mother made. She soaked hard boiled eggs in pickled beet juice until they were dyed magenta clear to the yoke. The tangy taste was Easter itself. When I'm away my thoughts turn to my family, my compass needle always pointing toward home.

A parade of letters from home keeps my attention grounded in Inglewood and southern California, and I respond to them with longing and affection.

I remember the good times we used to have going to the Wich Stand (A drive-in restaurant) *then the Liemert* (theater) *afterwards. Once in a while after that we would have a soda. To Charline and me, that was the best. If I can make a home half as good as ours, I'll be happy.*

At home, my father has planted a lemon tree that has already begun to blossom. To me the fragrance of lemon and orange blossoms is the scent of California. We used to drive through the citrus groves in Covina and Pomona, the intoxicating perfume of the blossoms spilling out over the roads. As interesting and exciting as the east coast is, it can't compare to my California memories.

After my folks send me my picture album, I spend hours looking at the photographs, all of them depicting good times at home---a group of us posing on the sands at Manhattan Beach, me with my dog in the mountains at Charleton Flats, pictures of our street and yard, my friends smiling and grinning at the camera.

Those pictures of home looked so good. Even though I'm having a good time here at Langley and New Jersey, I still long for my California, my Inglewood, and my home.

* * *

With our radar course at Langley Field winding down, choices need to be made. Being an instructor is possible, or I could go on with the men. One other option is to apply for radar patrol work in B-24s over the Pacific. It would be much safer than participating in bombing raids. Becoming an instructor would please my parents, but I would go nuts living that life. More action, not the perilous kind like combat flying, but being active, learning new skills and going new places would suit me better.

The war ending in Europe affects my plans. I definitely want to stay with the group as I have bonded with them.

Something is "in the breeze," but I don't know what it is. Perhaps we'll be assigned to B-29s or to medium bombers like the B-25 or A-26. According to our captain, rank will play a part in where we go. As there are only four 1st lieutenants in our group, I should get my choice. Perhaps California could be one of my options, but in the Air Corps, the situation is always fluid and confused.

As the days ripple by, knowing what to expect after Langley Field is a mystery. Now that the European war is over, the radar sets we mastered here, the APS-15s, are largely obsolete, having only been used in that theater, not the Pacific. We'll have to learn to operate more advanced sets. One base where we could get this training is at Williams Field near Chandler, Arizona. As the field's location is only a short trip from home, I'm all for it. Rumors certainly point to that possibility, but we know they are like soap bubbles, popping into nothing at the slightest whim of a commanding officer.

Now that the war is winding down, a point system has been devised for being discharged from the service. If a man has enough points, he is not automatically out, especially if he is essential---like radar operators. Points are based on years of service and time overseas as well as medals earned. I have 66 points, just 19 points short of what I need. Getting out of the service now is a distinct possibility in the near future.

The captain in charge of our training group calls me into his office. The burly but pleasant officer still suffers from the hurt of losing his first child during child birth. We had all expressed our sympathy for his loss. He asks me to sit down in a chair opposite his desk. "If you'd like to be an instructor here at Langley, it's yours Stevens."

I'm hesitant.

"You want to think it over. We'd be glad to have you."

"I appreciate the offer," I respond, "but I think I'll just go with the group."

"Well, good luck."

What is the right decision? Perhaps going on with the men just because they have become my good friends will lead me into a combat tour in the Pacific. Staying here as an instructor would keep me safe. Then again, the war in the Pacific might end soon. It's a gamble.

The word is finally official. I and the group will be sent to Williams Field, Arizona, the closest to home I've ever been stationed. I'm ecstatic! We'll be training there for over a month. As of yet we don't know how or when we'll get there.

In short order the questions are answered. We leave right away and have six days to reach Arizona by rail via Cincinnati and Chicago. Since we have so much time I plan to stop in Indiana to see my grandfather whom I have not seen since I was a small child and hardly remember. I consider it a rare opportunity to satisfy my curiosity about him.

My good friend, Roger Graef, will go with me part way as his home is in Portland, Indiana. He is an all around nice guy, and we think alike about most matters. Friendly and pleasant, he's taller than I am with thick dark hair and a face that always looks burnished and fresh. His wife is pregnant, so he wants to be with her, even if only for a day or two. We'll arrive in Cincinnati at 0800 then take a train from there to Richmond, Indiana. I'll then go to Dunrieth where my grandfather lives and Roger will go on to Portland. A few days later we'll meet at the La Salle Street Station in Chicago where we'll take the Rock Island to Tucumcari, New Mexico, then the Southern Pacific to Phoenix. It's a grand plan, and we hope it works.

A Visit with My Grandfather

Farms and fields flicker by as the train rolls across the table-flat farmland of Indiana. It was a rash decision, this trip. At Langley Field I had decided to stop by my grandfather's house in Indiana on my way to report for duty at Williams Field, Arizona. The officers at Langley Field, Virginia had given us more than ample time to reach our destination, plenty of extra hours for a side trip.

I had always wanted to see my grandfather, my Grandpa Weeks, but from my home in California he was always too far away. It is now 1945, and I am 20 years old. I haven't seen him since I was two. I glanced at several snapshots of him in his later years, but I have no clear vision of him. My plan is just to show up, arrive at his doorstep unannounced, a surprise for us both.

All that I knew about him I learned from my mother. She presented him as a strong man of great virtue. According to her, his strength of character nearly equaled Abraham Lincoln's. She extolled his bravery in a story about his chopping wood. The axe glanced off the block and sliced into his foot. He had borne the pain superhumanly insisted my mother, demonstrating his coolness and courage. She may have told me this as an example to stop me from whining or crying about some small discomfort, but I marveled at his manliness.

By the time the train approaches Richmond, Indiana, where I get off, the gathering clouds coalesce into a dark ominous threat. At the station the rain pours, hard slanting lines of it pounding and dancing in the street. I wait it out in the depot's shelter. I'll have to take a bus from here to Dunreith where my grandfather lives.

Now on the bus, the shower over, we rumble through the countryside. The corn and wheat fields, pastures, old white farmhouses and silos, cows, sheds, fences and tractors are the source of my roots. My mother and father as well as their fathers and mothers were all born and raised on Hoosier farms. I was the first in my family line to be born in California. I feel drawn to Indiana as a place where a person might live a good honest life close to the soil and nature. I suppose one day of stacking hay, cleaning out barns or milking cows would cure me of that longing.

Grandpa Weeks doesn't farm anymore. Instead he lives in a small rural village. I'm not sure what he had done for a living, but I know he's retired. I had heard that he worked for the road department occasionally, depending on what political party was in power at the time. He'd been a teacher once. According to my mother he'd shunned the outhouse at the school for fear that some of the rowdier kids would topple it over with him in it.

Dunreith is only a collection of a few white clapboard houses set along short streets without sidewalks. The town is so small I have no problem locating the right address. My stomach flutters with anticipation as I walk along the uneven asphalt. Perhaps I shouldn't be doing this. It's brazen of me not to warn them.

Dressed in my officer's uniform, I walk up several wooden steps to the large front porch. Two old chairs and a scrawny potted plant are all that occupy it. I knock on the front door. An older man with thinning hair opens it cautiously, not knowing who I am, a quizzical expression on his face.

"Hi Grandpa. I'm Norman, your grandson. I dropped by to see you. I hope you don't mind."

"Well, come on in," he says. "My goodness, I certainly didn't expect to see you. Viola! Look who's here. It's Charles Norman, Pauline's boy."

Viola, his present wife hurries to the door. "Why land's sake. How nice to see you," says Viola. "Oh, we're so happy you're here. Come on in. Can you stay awhile?"

"I'm on my way to Arizona," I explain. "They gave us an extra day to make the trip, so I thought I'd stop by here since I haven't seen you for so long. I know this is sudden, but I didn't know any other way to do it. I didn't have time to let you know."

"That's all right," says Viola. "You can stay a spell, can't you? Will you stay for supper and spend the night?"

Relieved and basking in their Midwestern hospitality, I accept their offer of an overnight stay.

"Could you use a glass of water, Norman?" asks Viola. "I bet you're thirsty from all that travelin'."

"That would be nice. My throat's really dry."

I follow her to the kitchen where she brings up fresh water from an old-fashioned hand pump mounted on the sink counter. She works the squeaking handle up and down, the clear well water pouring from the spout. She hands me the glass. The water tastes cool and fresh. I thank her.

I'm amazed that they don't have indoor plumbing. I didn't know anyone lived like this, especially my own grandparents. I try not to show my concern. I had always simply turned a faucet handle and let the water flow. I thought that's what all people did, that pumps were relics of a bygone age. We used to study diagrams about how they worked in my high school general science class, but we never saw a real one. I feel like I'm living in the last century, in the days of my grandfather's youth.

Later I ask to use the bathroom.

"The outhouse is out back," says my grandfather. "Come on. I'll show you where it is."

I follow him out across a sparse lawn and through the shade of several large trees.

"There it is."

"Thanks," I say, looking at the old wooden structure.

I had used these in campgrounds, but those were considerably grander than this weathered shack. I pull open the buckled door and peer in at the one-holer. Once inside, I attempt to pull the door shut, but it's warped so much that it leaves a crack almost two inches wide. The light pours through it, and consequently, I can see a small section of the scene outside, a long narrow strip framing part of the yard, trees, the highway with cars speeding by and a railroad. I'm glad for the opening because it allows fresh air to cut into the ripe smell inside. A Sears catalogue rests beside me. Cobwebs soften the shadowed corners high above me. I remember stories my mother used to tell me about using an outhouse at night on the farm. How once she felt something cold on her bare bottom, and it turned out to be the nose of a curious weasel.

While using the facility a freight train storms by billowing steam and black smoke, the sound deafening, the ground and outhouse vibrating. I enjoy the drama as it unfolds through the slit, the train dashing through my narrow view of the outside.

First the water pump and then the outhouse. I begin to feel sorry for them, living so primitively while most people in the United States get hot and cold water out of shiny faucets and use flush toilets in comfortable rooms within their houses. Even in the snow and the rain my grandfather and his family had to charge outside to this reeking and inhospitable setting to take care of their common needs. I suppose others in the Midwest live this way, but my grandfather is my blood relative.

After a sandwich for lunch, Grandpa Weeks and I sit by ourselves in the wicker chairs on the front porch. I observe him carefully. He's slimmer than and not as tall as I had imagined, only an inch or so taller than I am. His sparse hair is nearly all gray and appears uncombed, as though he only uses his hand to lay it back. His face is unremarkable, somewhat plain with a prominent nose.

I notice physical characteristics that he passed on to my mother and then to me, especially the nose.

"We don't know much about the war except what we read in the papers," he says. "What is it you did?"

"I'm a bombardier," I answer. "I flew in bombers out of England, over Germany and the occupied countries. My job was to drop the bombs."

"We've heard about that. Must have been pretty dangerous. Did you have any close calls?"

I tell him a few stories, but I discern through his eyes and his expressions that he doesn't really understand. How could he? I had the same problem with my parents. They listened intently, but did not comprehend. No one could, except for those who had had the same war experiences. I had learned to expect no more.

Changing the subject, he begins to tell me about Jenny, my mother's mother, who died soon after my mother was born. He remarried, this time to Viola who bore two children, Marian Faye and Jessie who is in the army somewhere.

"A friend of mine asked me one day if I would like to meet the sweetest, prettiest girl in the world," he says. "He told me she had dark hair, deep lovely eyes and a personality to match. I said, I'd love to meet someone like that. He told me her name was Jenny Brenneman and that he would point her out to me when we saw her. Well, he did later when she was walking with a group of young women. I was dumbstruck. She was as cute as he said she was. He arranged for me to meet her, and that was that. I fell instantly in love with her. It wasn't long after that

that we were married. She was a wonderful wife, and I still miss her terribly."

"I'm really glad you told me that," I say. "I never knew anything about your courtship. I don't know much about her short life either, only what little my mother told me."

I remember seeing an old photograph of Jenny, her dark hair short but curly, even a bit frizzy, her eyes full, rather wide, as though she were amazed at something--- like my mother's eyes. She's dressed in a turn-of-the-century outfit, modest, a high collar hiding most of her neck.

"Yes. She was the love of my life."

He is obviously still in love with her, the memory of her very much alive. He doesn't say anything about Viola. Not a word about how they met or how he feels about her. I get the feeling that she is only a woman of convenience, a companion, a person to bear his children. I begin to feel sorry for her, she who sits in the house this very moment while we on the front porch discuss his first passion.

Having finished telling me about Jenny, he begins relating a story about a local dentist.

"This unscrupulous dentist took advantage of the women who came into his office. He would put them out with nitrous oxide then fondle them right there in the dentist's chair. The temptation was just too much for him. Finally the women got wise to him and had him arrested. It just shows what some people will do."

I hardly know what to make of this. It is an interesting story, but where did it come from? Why would he choose to tell me about this?

"You know, I've heard that prostitutes make good wives." He says. "Once they get over their need for sex, or out of the situation they were in, they can settle down with a good man, remain faithful and become good mothers. Strange, isn't it?"

"I suppose that's possible," I respond. "But some of those women are pretty tough characters."

Why does he bring up these matters? Maybe he's just trying to make conversation or thinks as a man I would be interested in them. But I don't expect subjects like this coming out of my grandfather. Otherwise he seems quite wise to me.

In the afternoon he takes me in his car to visit many of my relatives, none of whom I had met before. All of them are still farming like my grandparents used to. All of them are glad to see me. Uncle Levi greets me, his overalls swelling over his prominent belly. The scent of hay and sour manure is in the air. "So you're Pauline's boy. My, my." No one calls me by my name. I'm "Pauline's boy."

Grandpa takes me to New Castle where he had lived before and shows me where my mother and her mother were born. We pass by the white farmhouse where my father lived as a boy. Being here is like peering into a past I never knew.

The supper at my grandfather's house was tasty---pork chops, mashed potatoes and gravy and fresh peas--- and I slept well. We are on our way to Indianapolis in their old car. They're going to take me to my mother's cousin's place in town where they have real running water, the conveniences of indoor plumbing.

My Grandpa Weeks is no Abe Lincoln. Although he diminished a bit in stature as I reacquainted myself with him, I still like him and feel close to him. I should have known better than to place him on a pedestal as my mother had. Of course I'm seeing him now as an old man, not as he was in the vigor of his youth. He may have been more imposing as a healthy young man. I suppose, after all, that he was an ordinary man, but a very nice one, simply doing what men generally do, earn a living and raise a family.

I'm still appalled at their living conditions, my own kin living so basically. As impulsive as it is for me to visit them, I'm glad I'm doing it. Not only am I learning about my grandfather but about myself and my tenuous roots that burrow into the Indiana soil.

An Introduction to Williams Field

Our barracks at the Shellbank section of Langley Field, built upon a foundation of crushed shells and muck dredged up from the bay, were stark, but the palatial brick barracks for the permanent officers were surrounded by velvet green lawns and venerable trees. Virginia was green and lush, a state of marshes, rivers and verdant forests. So were the farms and open country of Maryland, Delaware, Pennsylvania and parts of New Jersey that sped by the train windows on my many trips north.

As we travel west from Chicago the view from our Pullman window is quite different. We roll through the sparse, mesquite dotted plains of west Texas, the colorful but bare hills of New Mexico and the deserts of Arizona, the landscapes becoming more and more arid. Each click of the train wheels over the rail joints seems to suck more moisture out of our bodies.

This time, going to a new base will not be as tense since most of the men going with me are my fast friends from Langley Field. I'm upset though that Menke is not among them, having been sent to another base. I had enjoyed going to his home in New Jersey where they treated me like one of the family. I wanted to do the same for him in California with my family.

Williams Field near Mesa, Arizona is not far from Phoenix, square in the middle of the Sonoran Desert. To temper the dry desolation of the place the base is spruced up with a patchwork of lawns, hardy shrubs and ranks of young date palms. A row of the trees stands by our earth-toned, two-story barracks, giving us a touch of green, a bit of life. We'll have to get used to the dry air and the intense summer heat that quivers over the barren landscape. Out on the flight line silver B-24s gleam and shimmer in the sun. At least the base provides a large, blue swimming pool where we can cool off.

Soon after we arrive, the accounting officer summons some of us to his office and informs us that we have been absent without leave, AWOL. We explain to him that our orders clearly gave us six days to make the trip, that we had reported on the date indicated. "That doesn't matter," he says, a grim, no-nonsense look clouding his face, "You were to get here as fast as you could by the rail routes indicated in the orders. We're not giving you a couple of days off for a little paid vacation." Graef and I look at each other, dumbfounded. We had taken two days to visit family in Indiana, thinking we had plenty of time, that the arrival date printed in our orders was when we were supposed to report. He scribbles something down with a flourish of his pen, locks his eyes on us, and threatens to dock our pay.

I had never been AWOL. Only lazy, irresponsible soldiers did that. I had never even thought about going AWOL. Now that I'm being accused of it I'm beginning to feel guilty, yet at the same time, there is a secret little thrill in it---that I had been bold enough, although I hadn't meant to, to break the rules. I remember how the ne'er-do-wells in high school sauntered into the classrooms with their fiery red truant cards after ditching school--- how they smirked and obviously enjoyed the attention. Maybe I feel a little like that.

Now that I'm in the West, right next to California, my thoughts are naturally about home. If I schedule my time just right I might get to Inglewood for at least a day and a half this weekend. It would be a quick trip, but it would be worth it. I know by now though that the Air Corps is too fickle for me to count on it.

Soon after we arrive, Roger Graef, my traveling companion, and I take a bus into Phoenix, about thirty miles away, just to see the town. We stroll up and down the griddle-like streets, but soon grow weary, the merciless heat melting our resolve. We decide to look up Mary Lou, a girl I had known at Inglewood High School who had moved to Phoenix. She was always very friendly, and I knew she would be glad to see us. She's surprised when we arrive at her doorstep, but is her usual buoyant self. Her short brunette hair frames her freckled face. Perky and bouncy by nature she exudes an optimism that attracts people to her. We forget about the heat and have a great time talking and catching up with each other. "Hey, you know Artie Shaw is coming to town," she says. "You guys should come back then, and we could go dancing. I'll get a girl for Roger." We promise we will.

As I feared, the base commander decides to spring the orientation for our group earlier than scheduled, making it impossible for a trip home. I had hoped to bring Roger Graef, Jack Perry and Herb Plever home with me. Jack, tall and lanky, is a Harvard graduate and always impresses me with how much he knows. Herb is a small guy from New York and is a heck of a lot of fun, as well as being razor-sharp bright. I'm very disappointed we won't be able to go.

We are to start our classes in just a few days and will complete our training on July 21st, about one month total. Many of our flights will take us over California, closer and closer to home---near and yet so far. Flying directly over my house is my ultimate goal.

On the days that follow we find respite from the searing heat in the base swimming pool. The penetrating Arizona sun has already scorched my skin a brownish pink, the cool pool water soothing the sting. We play water polo, four on a side, hurling the ball, splashing water everywhere, shouting and gulping chlorinated mouthfuls. We keep at it until we quit from sheer exhaustion.

They don't dock our pay for being late, at least not yet. Perhaps they'll be lenient or maybe they'll forget all about it. We receive our travel pay, and I have enough left over to send $120 home.

The orientation takes place on a day that the

temperature reaches 111 degrees, the monotonous talk of the administrators combined with the stifling heat nearly putting us to sleep. I'm appointed as a flight leader in charge of eight men. Langley Field sends me a note that I received a superior rating from them. Because of it, the possibility of being an instructor opens up here and becomes one of my options. We top off the day at the air-cooled base theater by watching "Back to Bataan," a flag-waving movie about the war in the Philippines starring John Wayne and Anthony Quinn. We hated the super-patriotic films designed as propaganda, but they served a purpose in bolstering civilian morale.

Before We Fly

═══════════════

Sitting with the others in a room full of tablet arm chairs, I listen to the instructors lecture about radar bombing with the APQ-7 or "Eagle" model, the newest set in the Air Corps. The whirring air-conditioners make little impact on the heat, but the subject is so interesting I don't mind the discomfort. The "Eagle" is so secret that we have to lock up our notes in a vault when we leave classes, never being able to take them to our barracks for study. Even when we learned about the intricacies of the top secret Norden bombsight at Midland, we could always take our class notes with us. Why should one be treated more secretly than the other? There is a certain satisfaction in possessing a secret---having information about equipment that very few people are allowed to know.

I also learn that we'll be flying radar missions next weekend, blowing to confetti any chance of my going home. I'm disappointed about not seeing my family and friends, especially my girlfriend who has just graduated from high school. I sent her an armful of red roses, but being away for months now, I want to see her. I also planned to take some of the guys home with me. Perhaps the following week.

Splashing through the cool water of the pool during physical training, I'm proving to the instructor that I can swim twenty-five yards. I'm not as good at swimming as some of the other men, but I can churn my way through the pool, my arms flailing, water flying everywhere, the sound of my thrashing like an old fashioned washing machine. I complete the twenty-five yards then they test me for fifty. I have to show them that I can dog paddle, swim the breast stroke, side stroke and back stroke. Finally I must tread water for two minutes without sinking. We swim until we're exhausted, but at least we're out of the heat.

Roger, Herb and I book a hotel room in Phoenix so that we can stay in town Saturday afternoon and night as well as Sunday. After settling in our room at the Adams Hotel, Roger and I walk out to Mary Lou's place. Her mother is kind enough to serve us a fiery chili dinner with corn bread, a real treat and a change from the blander fare served in our mess halls. Hungry, as we always seem to be, we devour several bowls each. Full and ready to go, our mouths humming with the spicy chili, we're off to dance to the music of Artie Shaw.

Many couples shuffle about the dance floor, but it's so spacious that it's never crowded. We sometimes box step close to the famous band leader, swaying to the tempo of his swing music, his band sounding infinitely better in person than on his records. I have a stack of his platters at home that I often played. In the front row, behind white-fronted music stands, saxophones blare, their polished brass reflecting and distorting the lights. Trumpets and trombones are behind them, a bass player standing at the side. Vibrations from the instruments ripple through our bodies. A handsome man with parted, slicked-back hair, Artie Shaw is the "King of the Clarinet." Now and then he solos, his tones mellow, his expression and gestures at one with the music. We have a great time keeping step even if the beat of "Begin the Beguine," the piece that made him famous, is confusing. But "Stardust", "Moon Glow" and "Frenesi" are more our style. Artie Shaw is also famous for his many marriages, presently being married to the actress Ava Gardner.

Exhausted from dancing, we're back at Mary Lou's house slurping cold, ripe watermelon. We leave the house with the sweet taste of the melon on our lips.

By the time Roger and I wake up in our hotel room the sun is streaming through the tattered curtains. Still groggy from the lateness of returning to the hotel, we slowly dress and wander aimlessly along the Sunday-empty streets of Phoenix. As we are walking two young women begin strolling with us. "We have a car," they say. "Would you like to go bowling?" We have nothing better to do, so we go with them, bowling just enough to be friendly. They're very nice, but we have to leave them to return to the field.

The bus headed for the field is packed, every seat

taken, others crammed into the aisle. Rather than trying to force ourselves on the crowded bus, we decide to try the open road. Motorists take pity on us, and they get us back to the base in good time.

* * *

I look up at the pastel blue skies of Arizona, the air so clear that every object is distinct, the nearby mountain peaks especially sharp. The dry heat is intense, but I'm getting used to it. Now and then dust devils, like miniature earth-colored tornadoes, move silently across the desert floor. Sometimes they graze our base, whirling dust, twigs and paper into a frenzy. They are fascinating to observe, watching their growth and wondering where their erratic paths will take them. I suppose I identify with them, wondering where my life will take me.

I'm back in the pool now, still aching from yesterday's land calisthenics. They work us to the point where we think we're going to drown, taking all the fun out of being in the pool. One exercise today is diving off the high board. Luckily I had some experience with it. While I recovered from a broken arm in high school, my cast finally off, the coaches suggested I swim every day to strengthen my flaccid arm. Kindly, soft spoken Coach Badenoch encouraged me to learn to dive from the high board. "If you walk out to the very tip of the board, let your toes hang over the edge, lift your arms over your head into the diving position then let yourself fall forward, you'll make a perfect dive." With trepidation I climbed the ladder and walked out on the board. My God it was a long way down! I followed directions, held my body rigidly then fell forward. In seconds my pressed hands knifed into the water. I plunged a long way under the surface but soon bobbed up, exhilarated that I had done such a thing. I tried it again and again until I was confident.

Some of the permanent ground officers are in the pool with us today. I watch them as they topple, one after the other, off the high board. Some are pale and hesitant, obviously terrified. I feel for them, because I know how I once felt, but, at the same time I feel smug and superior because I can easily do it.

The physical training instructors also make us jump in the pool with our pants on. We slip them off with great difficulty, tie knots at the cuffs then swing the wet pants above the water to fill them with air. They act as a temporary float that could be used in an emergency.

The next day I'm running a cross-country course of a mile, sweat pouring off me in the searing heat, my lungs struggling for air, my shoes pounding the hard earth. We all finish, but our throats have been scoured by the oven-like air so that we can hardly swallow. Even a half hour afterwards our heads are pounding, a steady rhythm like a drum beat. On this base we're always thirsty, tanking up on water at every opportunity. Physical training is much more demanding here than at Langley Field where most of us got out of shape. If the PT instructors don't kill us, we'll probably be the better for it.

Most of us relax in the evening at the base movie theater watching "Thrill of a Romance" starring Van Johnson and Esther Williams.

The following night we have some rare entertainment on the base. In all the time I had been in the service, even overseas, I had never been entertained by any kind of group or show. Druke and Shaw are a two-piano team who play mainly classical works by Rachmaninoff, Debussy and Strauss. Finished with the older masters they slide into Gershwin with his "Rhapsody in Blue" followed by rumbas and sambas, even the "Tiger Rag." They also beat out their rendition of "La Cucaracha." We fill the auditorium with the thunder of our applause.

Tomorrow we fly.

Up in the Air

Searching the vastness of the desert night, I look for a checkpoint to estimate our position. I'm by myself in the nose of a B-24 with my maps, a small light, my E6B computer, a remote radar scope and the drone of the plane's four engines. I'm navigating by pilotage, comparing what I see on the ground with what's on my maps. Tonight I'm looking for luminous patterns of lights below, bright or dim, indicating the size of cities. I keep my reading light off except to briefly check my maps, my eyes having to adjust to the darkness and the detection of even the faintest lights ahead. I'm alone with the night, suspended in a star-scattered blackness, lulled into a sense of well being and peace, as though I'm part of it all, part of the universe. My partner, Herb Plever, is operating the radar in a small space just behind the pilots. Tomorrow night we'll switch places.

At times I see no lights at all, only a dark void. It reminds me of our night flight over the Atlantic to

England months ago, the same black nothingness. We had taken off tonight from Williams Field at 2030, climbed to 14,000 feet, then headed for Kingman, Arizona. Our route after Kingman will take us to Boulder Dam, Las Vegas, Nevada, to the Salton Sea near Calipatria then to Ajo, Arizona and back to the field. I'll fly over California for the first time on a regularly scheduled operation. I had flown over England, Germany and the occupied countries many times, but only once over my home state. That was when I rode along with the Navy guys on their Avenger torpedo bombers as far as Palm Springs. The flight tonight is smooth except for turbulence over the higher mountain ranges. Even though the peaks are far below they influence the weather with their tricky currents. Despite the darkness and the lack of good checkpoints we hit all our targets, landing at 0130 after a five-hour flight.

The following night Plever and I reverse positions, our plane flying the same route as the night before. Even at 12,000 feet the desert air is still warm. Unfortunately the radar set generates heat, and the plane had been sitting on the sun-drenched tarmac all day as well, gradually transforming it into a solar oven. My maps stick to my sweaty arms and wrists, my oxygen mask covering my nose and mouth adding to my discomfort. I strip down to the waist, something I had never done before in flight. The glow of the radar screen casts an eerie light on my bare chest.

I sit in front of the radar screen, watching the cursor move hypnotically back and forth like an electronic windshield wiper, illuminating a replica of the land before me. Unlike the APS-15 radar sets we used at Langley Field that swept in a full circle, the APQ-7 scans only a small area of a circle straight ahead of us, like a piece of pie, the sweep covering a narrow arc in great detail. It's so sensitive that it outlines railroad tracks and parts of highways. I easily find the Salton Sea as it shows up beautifully on the radar screen as a large black space, a dusky ink blot, its shores traced in electronic detail. Again we return very late.

With a heavy dose of flying, ground school and physical training, we're constantly busy with little time to relax. It reminds me of our grinding regime as cadets when we cherished even five minutes of free time. I can remember grabbing those three- minute naps.

We're flying every night now. Tonight we fly to Yuma, Arizona then to the Salton Sea and San Diego. We fly back via Parker Dam on the Colorado River and Phoenix. At each place we have a target to "bomb." A thin sea fog covers San Diego like a diaphanous veil, the city lights beneath it casting an ethereal glow. I look at it in awe, never having observed a sight quite like it.

* * *

Howling among the barracks and thrashing the date palms, a dust-laden wind lashes the field. The thick grit sometimes obscures the barracks next to us. But the wind finally abates, and we're cleared for flying.

We roar down the runway in the late afternoon,

daylight beginning to fade. Just as our plane clears the ground we lose an oil line on the number four engine, preventing us from obtaining full power. Luckily we're in a stripped down version of the B-24 and carry no bombs or extra fuel. If this had been a takeoff in combat we would have plowed into the earth, burst into a spectacular fireball and wound up in a smoldering pile of twisted aluminum. Not having full power, we barely gain altitude. Our plane struggles only a few hundred feet above the ground. Oil spews out of the engine and leaves a thick trail of black smoke behind us. We're too low to bail out. The sooty smoke billows, and the engine grows hotter and hotter. I'm sweating beneath my flying suit, and it's not just from the heat. My God! Did I survive all those bombing missions just to crash in the Arizona desert? The pilot tries to gain altitude, but he needs to feather the propeller so it'll stop turning and tearing up the engine. Would he have enough hydraulic pressure to do it? The engine is about to burst into flame. I'm praying silently, but finally the pilot controls the prop. We circle low around the field once then mercifully set it down. The squeal of the tires as they kiss the runway is a sweet, sweet sound. We taxi to the ramp. Once out of the plane, somewhat unsteady on our feet, we look up at the misbehaving engine, its shiny aluminum cowling slick with oil.

Much later, they assign us to another plane. In revving up the engines, the pilot discovers the magneto on the number two engine is not functioning, so the plane is unable to fly until it's repaired. Discouraged, we gather our equipment and crawl out of the plane. There will be no flying for us tonight.

It's late now. We stop by the midnight mess then back to the barracks for a good night's sleep, glad we're still alive.

Wings over Brett Street

═══════════

A line of light pulses back and forth on my radar scope, illuminating my target at Tucson, Arizona. In a few more minutes the "bomb" will be released. Actually we're camera bombing, the photos later to be analyzed by a staff at the field for accuracy. We had already made some runs on a few towns along the Mexican border before "attacking" the airfield at Tucson. Once the bombing run is completed we'll head back to Williams Field.

One of our turning points is a high, rugged mountain peak called Old Baldy. We fly at about 10,000 feet, clearing it with little to spare. As it reflects a strong echo, we have no problem picking it up on the radar screen. Ominous thunderheads rise all around us, huge towers and turrets of clouds rising almost into the stratosphere, dangerous and beautiful at the same time. Showing up as fuzzy bright spots on our scopes, the tempests are easy to avoid. Even though we fly in the clear air around them, turbulence, like invisible hands, shakes our plane roughly.

Captain Schultz, the CO of our section, is our pilot today. He's a skilled pilot as well as a great guy. My instructor is Lieutenant Gadwah, a former navigator and radar snooper with the Fifth Air Force. Patient and thorough, he's the best navigator I have ever worked with, and I'm lucky to have him as my teacher.

* * *

I have the Kaiser Steel Mill at Fontana lined up in my radar scope and am about to approach the bomb release point when our number one engine conks out and our number two engine begins throwing oil. Our concerned pilot decides to head for home right in the middle of my bomb run. He banks the plane sharply to the left, abruptly enough that I can feel the G-forces, and heads back for Williams Field. We fly directly over March Field in Riverside where I think we ought to land if we're in trouble, but the obstinate pilot wants to try for our home base. I was having good runs, hitting targets at Blythe and Lake Elsinore before our engines failed. We were supposed to go to San Juan Capistrano and the Salton Sea, but we have to cancel them. We fly out through the San Gorgonio Pass, Mt. San Jacinto on our right and Mt. San Gorgonio on our left, then out across the deserts, hoping our oil-leaking engine won't quit.

We had also lost an engine the day before. From my position in the nose I had a good view of the engines and noticed the problem. I called on the intercom.

"Navigator to flight engineer."

"Yeah, go ahead."

"Hey, oil is streaking over the cowling of number three engine. There's some thin smoke trailing out of it too."

"Roger. We'll take a look at it."

The pilot promptly shut down the engine and feathered the prop. I began to fear that the B-24s at Williams Field were not very well maintained.

* * *

Several days later we're ninety-two miles off the Baja California coast when our engines begin to sputter and cough. We can see nothing but water in every direction, only the hazy blue Pacific. One engine begins to leak oil and leave a trail of white smoke. I'm tired of sweating out these planes, always being concerned about getting into nerve-wracking predicaments like this. As a precaution we all slip into our bright yellow Mae Wests, securing them tightly. If we have to ditch in the water, we'll be ready. I quickly plot a course for San Diego, the pilot turning the big ship around, hoping the engines would get over their fits. On the way to San Diego the pilot and the flight engineer calm the engines down, and the sailing is smooth once again.

After reaching San Diego we turn north along the coast towards Mines Field (later to become LAX) which is to be the next target on our route. If the engines act up again we're going to land at Los Angeles which is fine with me, but the engines continue to purr. Mines Field is only five miles from my home in Inglewood, the closest I have ever been to it in flight. Knowing that we would fly over Inglewood on our bombing route, I had alerted my parents to watch for us, even though we would be at least 12,000 feet high.

Swooping in over Long Beach, I'm on the bomb run for Mines Field. The moment after I yell "bombs away" I leave the radar set and scramble down into the nose with Herb. With the pilot's permission I take charge of the plane, guiding it with the Norden bombsight connected to the autopilot. By the time I dash into the nose we're at a position just west of the familiar Baldwin Hills. By manipulating the bomb sight, I gradually turn the plane around. I fly it towards Inglewood from the northeast then swing it around to the right. Another slow turn brings the plane in from the east. And there is my house! My wonderful house, 12,000 feet below us! The pattern of the streets including Brett Street, my street, is quite distinctive, and the house next door has a bright blue roof, so finding my house is easy. I gawk at it until it begins to fade out of view, that miniature Monopoly house down there where my parents and sister go about their daily lives, where most of my life has been lived--that speck of a house where I had grown from a seven-year-old boy to an eighteen-year-old young man going off to war. I picture every room, imagine the fragrance of cookies baking in the oven, hear the wind singing through the needles of the casuarina trees, feel the softness of my bed's warm covers as I sleep in my innocence.

I turn over the plane to the pilot, and we swing toward the southwest, heading for San Juan Capistrano, our next target.

In a letter the following day, my mother and father write that they looked up all afternoon until their necks and backs were sore, but they never saw me and finally gave up. I tell them that we would have been there earlier, but because of our engine trouble and the alteration of our route, we arrived very late.

* * *

I love flying over southern California, enjoying new perspectives on places I've known all my life.

This morning we fly to the El Toro Marine Base then take a run at the Lockheed Aircraft plant at Burbank. A solid deck of clouds, like a lumpy mattress, lies over Burbank, but on my radar scope I can see the Lockheed plant clearly. After "bombing" Lockheed we turn toward the east and fly over the mountains. Down below is Mt. Wilson with its silver telescope housings, both San Gabriel dams and barren Mt. Baldy without a trace of snow on it. We continue cruising over the San Bernardino Mountains, and I look longingly down on Lake Arrowhead and Big Bear Lake that I know so well. Patches of snow lie on the north slope of Mt. San Gorgonio, and as we fly toward Palm Springs we see snow tucked in the crags of Mt. San Jacinto. It's fun looking down on all the places that are so familiar to me.

After we land at Williams Field, I hadn't walked a hundred feet from the plane before the guys from the other flights that had flown the same route begin razzing me.

"Hey Stevens! I thought you were from sunny southern

California. All I saw down there was a bunch of clouds and fog."

I try to explain about the summer marine layer, but it's no use.

"Sunny California, my ass," they shout.

Wrapping It up at Williams Field

A scattering of blips lights up my radar screen. Which one do I want? Which one is the echo of the Lockheed Plant? Gradually I find what I think is it, release my "bombs" and hope for the best. I'm reasonably confident I've hit it. Burbank and Glendale are again covered with clouds.

On our way to other targets we fly over the San Gabriels and the mountain resorts. Near Big Bear in the San Bernardino Mountains a dark column of smoke from a forest fire rises over 13,000 feet, its currents jolting our plane as we fly through it. The acrid smell of smoke seeps into our plane through every small opening, the stench lingering long afterward. After "bombing" the airfield at Blythe and a packing plant in Phoenix our tires squeal on the runway at Williams Field.

At last the coming weekend seems free, possibly with enough time to go home. Scottie from our radar group, the only one I know who owns a car, whose home is in

Riverside, volunteers to take me and anyone else who wants to go.

* * *

I'm doing pretty good about not worrying too much about what happened. I get along well for a while, then it hits me all of a sudden. If I can just keep my mind on something else, maybe these feelings will be less and less frequent. I ate in the PX with some fellas at noon today. Well there was a girl in there that looked just like her. It startled me at first. Then I couldn't even finish what I was eating.

What I had hoped would be a wonderful time at home becomes a personal disaster. "We're so different Stevie," she says. "You're so calm, and I'm so nervous and emotional. I just think we should split up." I'm crushed. My life leaks out of me, leaving me deflated like a soft, withered balloon. The exciting world that I'm used to suddenly becomes dull and gray, a haze wrapped around everything. My family tries to cheer me up, telling me about their heartbreaks and how they got over them, but their words are to no avail. An emotional sink hole has opened up and swallowed me.

Several days later we have word that we'll get a fifteen-day furlough, starting in just a few days. At the end of the leave we'll all be sent to Herington, Kansas. I'll be far away from home again which might be just as well.

Our weekend leave over, I meet Scottie and his wife in Riverside for the trip back to Williams Field, first stopping at his mother's house for refreshments. She had lived most of her life in Glasgow, Scotland. Since I had visited Glasgow on one of my leaves, we had much to talk about. Short and slender, Scottie is older than most of us, crows feet already beginning to form around the outer corners of his eyes. He's the only one of our group who is married. Leaving just after midnight, we drive out on the desert at its coolest time. It's August though, and the desert is not only hot but humid, the warm sticky air mass creeping up from the Gulf of Mexico loaded with moisture and thunderstorms. By the time we reach Arizona, thunderheads rise ominously over the desert mountains. We stop at Salome for breakfast then continue to Tempe where Scottie and his wife have a room in the dorm of Arizona State College.

The barracks back at Williams Field are stifling. Our air-conditioning system barely functions as all our coolers are the evaporative type, dependent on water evaporating from wet "straw" packing, a fan blowing the colder air into our rooms. But the moist air reduces evaporation and thus the cooling. We can hardly breathe.

While we were gone a storm had ripped through our base, blowing off our door and plucking shingles from our roof. Telephone wires, billboards and a few trees are down. The guys who stayed on the base tell us that rain fell through blowing dust, converting the drops to thin mud.

I've had some time to contemplate where my decisions are taking me. I had declined to take an offer of becoming an instructor at Langley Field, choosing instead to stay with the group of men with whom I had trained, now my good friends. I had decided to travel with them here to Williams Field. We were becoming expert radar bombardiers and would be used on B-29 bomber crews for the all-out assault on Japan. It means going back into combat again, something I really didn't have to do, letting the pleasure of camaraderie with the men guide me into this situation. It would mean a resumption of that aching apprehension of facing disaster, watching the clear, high altitude air erupt with a thousand black bursts of anti-aircraft shells. It would mean more uttering of quiet dry-mouthed prayers, scanning the skies for enemy fighters. Would my muscles become as tight as guitar strings again? Would my bladder contract with pressure, my intestines writhe like serpents again? I had brought all of this on myself. It is as though I hadn't been thinking at all.

I'm not a natural fighter, a warrior, who thrives on action and danger, who feels most alive when challenging death. I'm a young man, caught up in a war, serving my country, but who looks forward to life and a future and being united with my loved ones again.

We have only one more flight, a short one to Grand Canyon. Having never seen it, I feel lucky to look down upon its magnificence from our plane. Our B-24 flies in wide circles over the yawning canyon, each circuit lowering our altitude. The closer we get the more we can see of the red, white and buff rock layers. The immensity of it is wondrous to behold. We've dropped our altitude so that we're almost even with the canyon's edge, the pine trees flying by. Over the northern rim we buzz the hotel, roaring only a few feet over its roof, undoubtedly startling the vacationers, rattling the rafters and sending the squirrels running for cover. Our pilot then decides he wants to fly down in the canyon. He aligns our plane with the length of the canyon then drops the nose down. I don't believe a four-engine bomber had ever done this. We're not far below the rim, but I'm nervous about flying down in here, never liking to take unnecessary chances. The canyon walls become a blur, the modern throbbing of our engines resounding from the ancient rocks. But I think more about our safety than the beauty of the canyon. Finally we lift out of it, gaining altitude for the flight home. I suppose the pilot wanted the notoriety of being skilled or courageous enough to fly a bomber down in such a famous place, something to tell his kids or his grandkids someday. It was an adventure, but I prefer pilots that are sensible. I'm glad to be back on the ground at Williams.

On the Plains of Kansas

═══════════

The Pullman car clicks over the rails as we pass through the wheat fields and small towns of Kansas, the rhythmic sound soothing yet melancholy. The trip had been long from Los Angeles after my leave at home from Williams Field. The train is almost an hour late, but the Rock Island locomotive is doing its best to make up time.

My mind is a kaleidoscope of thoughts, the pleasures and disappointments of my leave and the doubts about my future tumbling around in different shapes and colors.

The monumental event that happened while I was on leave was the dropping of the atomic bomb at Hiroshima on August 6th, 1945. Every paper carried photos of the great mushroom cloud rising over the utter destruction of the city. The use of the bomb was a horrible event, instantly killing over 90,000 human beings. How could Japan survive and carry on with the war? We all thought the Japanese would have to capitulate now. Only a few days later, on August 9th, another bomb devastated

Nagasaki. Surely that would convince them to quit. Then it was official; the Japanese surrender. On August 15th the agreement was signed ending all hostilities. More photographs appeared in the newspaper of the Japanese envoys dressed in black suits with top hats, as though they were from another era. The Japanese generals stood at attention with them on the decks of the USS Missouri in their military uniforms decorated with medals and gold braid.

Although the slaughter and maiming of the Japanese at Hiroshima and Nagasaki was a ghastly blow to mankind, the bombing may have saved the lives of millions of American and Japanese soldiers as well as civilians who would have perished in a full-scale invasion of Japan. Perhaps I would have been one of them.

But what does it all mean for me? It means the war is over, that I'm going to live. I'm going to survive the war and live a normal man's life. I'm jubilant like everyone else because, being human, I think about my own life, the carnage thousands of miles across the Pacific being relegated to the edges of my consciousness. That terrible event releases me from the possibility that I might die. The thought of it wells up in me like a great warm bubble.

I'm a full-fledged radar operator, but what do I do now? With the end of the war in Europe and now Japan so many changes are occurring in the military that we can't rely on getting any definite information about what lies ahead. They're sending us to Herington, Kansas, a staging area for overseas deployment, to join B-29 crews that have trained in Alamogordo, New Mexico. We are to be their radar operators. But why are they doing this when the war is officially over? Apparently, once plans have been put into motion they are hard to stop.

I finally reach the small town of Herington that at first appears not to have much to offer, only several blocks of two-story brick buildings. I can't imagine coming into it on a pass. What would I do? I'm surprised that the Rock Island station is so large, a two-story building constructed of rugged limestone blocks with the Rock Island logo on its end. At the station, I phone the airfield for transportation, the base being eleven miles outside of town. Shortly a small army truck picks me up. Once out of town we roll past fields and farms on land as flat as a billiard table with a few ripples here and there. Silver silos rise out of sorghum fields. I wonder about the layout of the base, what kind of quarters we'll have and most of all what my function will be.

Once we settle in we find that the movement of the B-29 crews from Alamogordo has been cancelled. We will not be joining these crews. Now what? The officer in charge promises we won't remain in Herington very long, but where we'll go from here is a mystery-- more unknowns to think about. I don't believe this officer any more than I do the others. Rumors are that we might transfer to El Paso, Texas or Tucson, Arizona, very near where we started.

The base at Herington is small and compact, making it easy to find everything. The sun is scorching during the day, and the nights are cool, but what annoy me most are the pesky flies that constantly nag us in the barracks. So many flies swarmed inside the Rock Island station when I arrived that I was glad to get out of it. Perhaps they're endemic in farming communities where there's plenty of animal dung and rotting refuse.

A large group of silver B-29s are on the flight line at the base, but apparently we are not going to fly in them. They're magnificent airplanes, but may or may not be a part of my immediate future.

* * *

The days pass without our learning any more about what we're going to do. We have meetings twice a day with our commander, but they never have anything new to say. Being here is like our sorry existence at Midland or Selman Field all over again. They don't know what to do with us. In the meantime we wait and pass the time sifting through rumors and keeping ourselves occupied playing pool and watching movies.

Finally they give us an opportunity to get our flying time in for our extra pay. Being up in the air again and actually doing something will be a relief. Since we have mainly B-29s on the field, I'm excited about flying in one. Down at the ramp, I check in at the flight office to find out what plane I'll be flying in. I'm disappointed to discover that I'll be flying in the only B-24 on the field, an old B-24E model called "Old Herringbone," named after our base that is affectionately known as Herringbone Army Air Base.

We are to fly one hundred miles west of Herington to another B-29 base at Walker, Kansas. Thunderheads are beginning to build, some of them looking very angry. We fly close to a potent storm, encountering the usual bumpiness and watching streak after streak of lightning zap from the clouds to the ground. Some of the bolts dart uncomfortably near us, close enough to startle me. I had never liked toying with thunderstorms, and I'm nervous about this one. Not only are we flying in an old decrepit B-24, but we have to contend with the storm's fury. Eventually we edge away from the black monster, making me feel much better.

We land at Walker and let a major get out, apparently on military business. We take off again, flying in wide circles around the airfield, looking down on the patchwork of wheat and sorghum fields below. After we have killed enough time, we land and pick up the major. His work finished, we take off for Herington.

Used to mechanical problems on B-24s, I'm happy that this flight appears to be flawless. As we reach Herington and settle into the approach for landing, the pilot informs us that something is wrong with the nose wheel. He can't get it all the way down, and he doesn't think it's going to lock in place. Two braces appear to be broken.

"I want you all to get in the waist behind the bomb bays," yells the co-pilot, over the roar of our engines. "Just as soon as our wheels touch the runway, I want all of you guys to rush back towards the tail. Maybe with your added weight we can keep that nose wheel up until we're about stopped, keep us from nosing in. Good luck!"

As soon as our tires screech on the runway, we all scramble back towards the tail. With our weight bearing down on the back, the metal tail skid starts dragging on the runway. I can see it and the shower of sparks and flame it leaves behind, the racket of its scraping deafening. We roll down the runway, keeping the nose wheel from touching, the fireworks display whipped up by our tail skid creating a spectacular show. As the pilot hoped, the nose wheel doesn't touch until we nearly stop. If we hadn't done what we did, we would have nosed in for a potentially bad accident. The base, having been warned of our problem, is ready for us. Red fire trucks with flashing lights are ready to spray foam. An ambulance and emergency trucks are not far behind. Men run out on foot to aid us or to see what's happening. We had used most of the runway as our braking power was limited, only a few feet being left at the end.

Being at Herington is not a bore any more.

Cousin Betty

The water takes my breath away. Used to the warm sun-heated swimming pools at Williams Field, this butt-freezing one shocks me. Fresh water from a deep well continuously flows into it then out at the other end, keeping it perpetually chilled. Despite its icy temperature, taking a dip is a relief from the heat and something to do.

Looking for something else to fill our time, to shake us out of our doldrums, four of us chose partners and play twenty-two straight games of pool. The pool balls click from 1900 until midnight. The matches are close, one side winning twelve, the other ten, the excitement of competition stirring our juices, jolting us out of our lethargy.

* * *

I lie on my bunk looking up at the ceiling boards, noting their grain patterns, wondering what I'm going to do next. I mull over the possibilities. Other than our daily meetings, the officers in charge have nothing substantial for us to do. Our routine is sleeping, eating, swimming, pool playing, letter writing and going to the base theater at night. We do nothing of military significance. Penning letters is difficult because there is little to write about.

For excitement I take my uniforms and underwear to the cleaners in town.

Since our future is so indefinite, I'm taking a chance that they'll not be finished before we leave. We might ship out at any time then I'd have to leave them behind. I walk down the main street of Herington, liking the town better than I did at first. The old brick buildings house the same kind of shops and businesses that larger towns have, just fewer of them. After walking I cool off in their small park, sitting in the dappled shade of a large, spreading tree. Nearby are a swimming pool and an obelisk-like monument honoring Father Padilla, a member of the Coronado Expedition who was killed by Indians he was attempting to convert. It is so peaceful today that it is difficult to imagine the violence that once occurred here.

* * *

Several days later, standing at the edge of a wheat field, I wait for a ride. The road where I hope to be picked up is little used and runs through isolated farm land. Sometimes ten minutes go by between cars. The sun beats down out of a clear hazy sky, and I'm beginning to sweat. It's peaceful here though, the wheat barely stirring in a light breeze with only the chatter of sparrows and the caws of crows breaking the silence. A car driven by a middle-aged woman roars by, but doesn't stop. She doesn't even look at me. I begin to wonder whether I'm ever going to get out of here. I'd had good luck with rides out of Herington and beyond, but now I'm stuck.

I'm on my way to see Betty, a kind of cousin, the lineage too complex to explain. She sometimes took care of my sister and me as kids, and we saw a lot of her when she lived in Los Angeles. When she married and moved to Manhattan, Kansas we lost track of her.

I'd had lunch on the way at Junction City, so at least I'm not hungry. Finally an old man, his gray hair flying, picks me up in his small truck. "I can take you as far as Fort Riley," he says. "That help you any?" "That'll be fine," I answer, glad to get out of this lonely spot. Luckily, at Fort Riley a lieutenant colonel gives me a ride all the way to Manhattan.

Betty of course is surprised when I call her from a hotel. I probably should have told her I was coming. Fortunately her house is only a few blocks away.

Even though she didn't expect me, she's glad to see me. I'm happy about this, because when I was younger I gave her a bad time with my teasing and silliness. For some reason I always felt bratty around her when I was a kid, and I remember how disgusted she was with me. She seems to have forgiven me for acting like the pill I was around her. Her short brunette hair frames her pretty face, her brown eyes deep and dark. Her husband is away in the service.

Her baby is asleep in his crib but soon wakes up. Betty

and I have a great time talking then riding around town, shopping and calling on people. Finally, after leaving the baby with her husband's grandmother, we drive to Junction City to see a movie. I hadn't driven a car in a long time, but Betty lets me have a turn at the wheel. Out of practice, I make turns "like an old woman," according to her.

She lets me sleep on her couch then I return to Herington, this time having better luck at hitchhiking.

* * *

Now that the war is over, most of us want to get out of the service as soon as possible, get on with our civilian lives. Rumors are rampant about when we'll be discharged and about the point system that will determine our eligibility. Having little else to do, I spend part of the day finding out as much as I can about this. Major Thompson who is in charge of us says he doesn't know any more about it than we do.

I then talk to a captain in the Combat Crew Headquarters. "You should be out in the very near future," he says. "Right now they're taking a census of how many want to remain in the military and how many don't. After they separate them, the ones with the highest point scores will be released. In a week or two we'll have much more information, and the discharges will come all of a sudden."

But does he really know or is he spreading rumors he has heard from others? I still don't know whether to believe him, but I feel buoyed by what he says. Perhaps Herington will be my last base.

The afternoon is warm when the base puts on a beer bust, barbeque and dance. Perhaps it's an attempt to shake up the dull routine of our days. We're all enjoying the cold suds and the tasty barbequed steaks. The dance, however, is like most I have attended on an army base---about one girl for every hundred men, or so it seems.

Keough and I go into town to pick up his cleaning, mainly for something to do. We ride in with Scottie and his wife who have their car with them. Instead of going directly into Herington, we drive out about fifteen miles the other direction to Council Grove. As we drive on to Council Grove Lake, I feel I'm in another state. It's a shimmering blue lake, so different from the flat farmland we're used to seeing. We cruise all the way around the lake in what they call the Flint Hills area. Oak and hickory line the rocky edges of the lake, small waves lapping the shore. I almost feel as though I'm like a free man on vacation rather than being in the army. I'm beginning to feel like a civilian.

Superfortress

From the first time I set my eyes on a B-29 Superfortress, I wanted to fly in one. I'd seen them from the air, gleaming silvery on the flight line below us and, from a distance, on our own ramp, but that's as close as I had ever been.

The plane seemed even more monstrous when we walked down to the flight line to board it this morning. Being in the shadow of that great wing was awesome, the impact of being so close to its massive size transforming us into Lilliputians. Rumors were that our group was to operate the radar on the 25 B-29s making a flight to Colorado Springs, but actually we're only to be passengers. Rather than practicing combat formations the planes will fly singly.

I thought we'd never leave the ground at take off, the heavy, lumbering plane using practically all the runway before it reluctantly became airborne. But now that we're up, the flying is smooth. I sit comfortably by one of the waist windows, watching the patchwork of fields roll slowly by beneath me. We're up at 10,000 feet where we normally use oxygen masks, but since the plane is pressurized, we don't need them.

Ours is the only plane that lands at Colorado Springs, the rest turning back to Herington. We glide in smoothly at Peterson Field, the headquarters of the 2nd Air Force. Our pilot, a full colonel, is the commander of the 383rd Bombardment Group stationed at Herington. He wants to know what's going to happen to his group. From the way he talks, he is as much in the dark as any of us about the near future and how we fit into it. He and our co-pilot, a Lieutenant Colonel, spend four hours in conference with the 2nd Air Force Commander.

While we wait, those of us who are along for the ride enjoy the cooler weather, a relief from the incessant heat of Kansas. We have a spectacular view of the jagged Rockies with Pike's Peak staring right at us. There's nothing for us to do here but chat, down a few Cokes and hang around the airplane.

After the conference, the pilots return, their faces grim. We'll never know why.

Its four powerful engines coughing into life, our plane taxies toward the runway for the return flight. Suddenly a turbo on the number 3 engine catches fire. Orange flames lick around its side. The tongue of fire flows back past the wing. It happens so quickly that I don't have time to react. The pilot responds immediately, cutting the engine. The fire gradually recedes then puffs out. I'm nervous about B-24s, now I'll have to add B-29s to the list. When we flew B-17s in combat we never had trouble with faulty engines or fires unless we were hit by the enemy, but the planes stateside seem to frequently break down. Perhaps it has to do with the quality of maintenance or the age of the aircraft.

After the pilot restarts the engine, happily no fire recurs. Once off the ground the plane flies smoothly, all four engines behaving themselves. We cruise at 230 mph, considerably faster than we flew in B-17s or B-24s. Because of the pressurization, the engine sounds are muted. It's so quiet we can talk to each other without shouting. We had to rely on our intercom to be accurately heard over the thunderous noise and vibrations of the B-17. We would have been cool in a B-17 at this altitude, but the temperature in the B-29 cabin is quite pleasant, almost warm. Our silky flight ends when we encounter clouds and afternoon turbulence. The Superfortress behaves like any other bomber in rough air, bouncing and bucking as it's buffeted by convection currents. We have no idea what the colonel found out at headquarters. Even the generals are confused.

* * *

Keough and I bounce along in the back of an army truck. He has been with me since Langley Field. A quiet, easy-going man, his eyes squint naturally, as though he looks far into the distance. He combs his lush hair back in a gentle wave, his complexion fair, his jaw square. The farther we travel, the harder the wooden benches become. We're on our way to Topeka for the weekend, hoping to take in the Kansas State Fair, (Some call it the Shawnee

County Fair). Ninety miles and a thousand bumps and jolts later we arrive in downtown Topeka.

We walk down the main street looking for a hotel room, but because of the crowds attracted to the fair, none are available. We don't worry much because we can always get a sack at the Topeka Army Air Base.

I'm surprised at how small the fair is compared to The Los Angeles County Fair at home. The wicked heat of the day is still with us as we stroll down the crowded midway, listening to the screams of the girls on the rides and the thuds of bumper cars. A Ferris wheel slowly turns, boys showing off to their girlfriends by rocking the seats. After our adventures in the air, the rides seem tame. I don't really know why we're here except to put some life into our weekend. We mosey on as a young man shows off his muscles by slamming down a large hammer, sending a metal object high enough to ring a bell. He struts away proudly.

After dark, we decide to watch the "Big Show" in the grand stand. Other than shooting a woman out of a cannon, the show seems only average. Maybe we're not in the mood for it. But that woman flying through the air and into the net is spectacular. That is really something. How did she endure the explosive charge that blew her out of that muzzle?

Exhausted at one o'clock in the morning, we wait at a bus stop for a ride back into Topeka. When a middle-aged couple offers us a lift, we gladly accept. As we ride in the back seat of their car, we ask them if they know of a hotel in town where we might stay.

"No, we don't know of a place off hand," the man says. "Why don't you come home with us? We have a back room with a bed in it."

"Oh you don't have to do that," I respond. "We'll find a place."

"But it's no trouble at all," he insists.

In the meantime, he drives past the center of town out toward the suburbs. Keough and I look at each other, concerned. We don't know these people. What do they have in mind? Are they just being nice or what?

With some apprehension, we accept their invitation. They turn out to be very nice, good-hearted people who have a son in the army. In a way, I think, we're a substitute for him. A large photograph of the young man stands in the living room and another one in the back room where we stay. Having a bed for the night is a great relief.

We sleep well then find they're preparing a breakfast for us, the tangy smell of sizzling bacon invading our room. Thinking we have imposed on them enough, we turn down their offer to feed us, thank them profusely and leave. As we walk away we think that maybe we should have stayed. They were cooking up a feast for us, were doing something special to please us. Why didn't we stay? I have a quirk in the soil of my psyche, planted long ago, like a seedling, by my mother that I shouldn't ever bother anybody, should never put people out, especially if they wanted to do something for me. The quirk pops up automatically. We leave with a sense of guilt, uneasy about having disappointed them. But we made our decision, and it's over. We finally find a bus stop and board a local bus for town.

Back in town, seeking refuge from the blistering heat, we duck into an air-conditioned theater and then a bowling alley. The rest of the time we spend in aimless walking, gawking and talking. By 2000 hours we hop on an army bus that will take us back to Herington.

From Kansas to Colorado

═══════════

After a thunderstorm, the air is cool and crisp, the base washed and fresh again. It's a relief to breathe pure air once more and get a break from the incessant heat, but we are still idle and at loose ends. I spend my day whacking ping-pong balls back and forth, ka-plunk, ka-plunk and listening to the clickity clack of pool balls colliding. At least there's always a movie to look forward to after dinner to help fill up the day.

Every time our commanders tell us they'll have news about when and where we'll be shipped, the promises pop like punctured balloons. Our only purpose in being sent here was to join B-29 crews that are now, for some strange reason, not coming. There is no use for us here. Even the base commander doesn't know what to do with us. The war has been officially over for a week, and the military, armed and ready for the final push on Japan, has nowhere to go. The discharge of all those men will take a while, so I'll have to wait.

At last we have a bit of news that seems plausible. Our commanding officer informs us that we'll leave in only two more days for Pueblo, Colorado. We are again to meet B-29 crews who have finished their training but lack radar operators. I have a distinct feeling that we'll be sitting around in Colorado just as we are here and so will those crews we are to meet.

The B-29 program is stymied throughout the country. Hardly a prop turns on a Superfortress any more. All that muscle with no place to use it.

I'm happy about traveling to Pueblo and being near the Rockies. It's only forty miles from Colorado Springs and a hundred and ten from Denver. I hope I'll have a chance to visit both cities. The news pulls me out of my lethargy. We're finally going to move and do something.

My good friends Herb Plever and Roger Graef are in Kearny, Nebraska where they are to meet crews from El Paso. More and more I'm separated from the men I met at Langley Field. Each time we make a move we're dispersed in different directions. They are the reason why I shunned being an instructor in the first place as I wanted to be with them, but now I'm more isolated from them than ever. My friends in Kearny later tell me the crews never arrive from El Paso. They are in the same predicament we are.

* * *

Our packed bags are all trucked to the Rock Island depot in Herington. We're actually going to leave. We'll travel all night in a coach, but at least we'll be on the move. I won't get much sleep, but I'll have fun chatting with the guys.

We arrive in Pueblo in the morning, haggard and exhausted. We had adjusted some of the musty seats in the chair car in an attempt to fashion some crude beds, but they were only mildly successful. No matter how we tried we couldn't get comfortable, only grabbing snatches of sleep amid the roar and rolling of the coach. The combination of our lack of sleep and arriving at a new base is a surreal experience, dreamlike and strange. Our new quarters swim around in our sleep-blurred vision but seem nice enough. The base is short of supplies, so we have no sheets on our beds. We'll have to make do by sleeping between army blankets, the wool ones that always irritate my skin, especially around my neck. They remind me of the wool trousers my parents made me wear to Sunday school when I was a kid, the ones that itched my legs unmercifully.

After a good night's sleep we're whole again, ready to resume military life. Our first jolt is that the commanding officers here don't know why we were sent to them. But I don't know why I'm surprised. The Pueblo base wires 2nd Air Force Headquarters, inquiring about what they should tell us. It's Herington all over again.

We have no real duty here. We sign in once per day then have time for ourselves with very little structure. They promise to provide flying time, perhaps in the fleet of B-29s stationed at the field, but I rarely see one take off. The same situation stifles other fields. What will they do with all this equipment and the thousands of men trained to operate it?

There are no crews for us to join here. But I ponder what might have happened if the war had continued and an invasion was launched against Japan. Following the path that I had chosen, I would have been a radar bombardier on a B-29 flying through Japanese flak and interceptors, right back in combat again. I might not have been so lucky this time. I had gambled that the war would end, and I had won, but I shudder when I think about what might have happened.

As a bulwark against inactivity and for a taste of civilian life, many of us sign up for courses at Pueblo Junior College. The program is launched as an agreement between the school and the base. I sign up for classes for three days a week, mostly in the afternoon. Part of the agreement is that the classes will take precedence over all the base duties except flying. I choose two classes, psychology and physics.

After riding two buses and a rickety street car I arrive at the small campus, most of it comprised of only two buildings, and ask directions to my classes. Sitting in tablet arm chairs in a real classroom with a blackboard and a civilian instructor is a real pleasure. The only disappointment is that all the students in the psychology class are from the base, uniforms all around me, just like in the barracks. The physics class is composed of a half dozen army men, three civilian boys and one girl. Again I'm disappointed. I thought more girls would be in the classes. I'm tired of being with men, yet here I am again surrounded by them. I yearn for the sweet sounds of female voices. As much as I enjoy the novelty of attending college classes, getting out of the service dominates my thinking. Being home again trumps my desire to be with my military friends.

I saw the headlines in the paper tonight, and it said something about discharging those who have been in the service over two years. Boy, I'm all for it. Some flight officers and second lieutenants on this field who have fewer points than I do are getting discharges. I think it is because they are pilots and less essential men. I think it's unfair since I've just done nothing for the past three months. That sure doesn't sound as though I'm essential. Maybe they will wise up one of these days.

Exploring Colorado and Other Matters

The day is sunny and warm despite a fresh dusting of snow on the Rockies. I never tire of gazing at the majestic peaks, today etched sharp and clear against a pristine blue sky. It's hard to believe that yesterday was cold, cloudy and miserable. Weather changes fast here. The mornings gradually become colder and crisper, prompting me to write a letter home requesting my winter uniforms that I had stored there. In a little more than a week we'll be required to wear only our winter uniforms on the base.

Later, five of us stand by the side of the road outside of Pueblo, hoping to hitch a ride north to Colorado Springs. A soft breeze rustles the bushes near us. We hold our thumbs up in the traditional way while the cars and trucks zoom by. Many kind people pick up service men, so we shouldn't have long to wait. Already a young man in a Ford is pulling over.

Arriving in Colorado Springs in mid-afternoon, we check in at the Alamo Hotel. The first order of business is finding a place to eat. Keough and I are always hungry. As we stroll around town looking for a restaurant two girls driving a Model A Ford hail us and ask us if we want a ride. They take us for a spin about twenty miles up into the foothills to Woodland Park. Once there we pause long enough for a beer and a burger at a rustic café. Sitting in a booth with fake leather cushions, we exchange patter in a clumsy attempt to know each other, a juke box belting out "Rum and Coca-Cola" on the other side of the room. One of the inquisitive girls annoys me by continuously asking me to take my hat off so she can check my hair. She's picky and shallow, and I immediately begin to dislike her. Why would she care what my hair looks like? I don't know what they were expecting, and I don't know what we were expecting. Finally they take us back to town, thank us for the beer and grub, and dump us.

About noon the next day we decide to take the ride to the top of Pikes Peak. We arrive at the cog-wheel train station on time, but discover we don't have enough money to pay for the tickets. Sadly we watch the train grind up the hill with a lot of happy people who are not broke. As the red train disappears up the steep tracks, Shepherd, another one of my friends from Langley Field, discovers a twenty-dollar bill under a flap in his wallet. It's too late, as the train now on its way up the hill is making its final trip of the day.

With our newly discovered wealth we decide to ride a

bus to Manitou where we can take the Cave of the Winds tour. At Manitou we board a stagecoach-like contraption drawn by two horses. The steeds gallop around the turns, churning up the dust, just as we have seen in cowboy movies. Hoofs thunder and the coach creaks. We pass close to the Garden of the Gods, hanging on, checking the strange red rock formations. At last we arrive at the cave entrance and are glad to get off the rickety thing.

We walk into the cool atmosphere of the cave with a guide and a bevy of other tourists. I'm overwhelmed with the dimly-lit formations, the stalactites, some massive, some delicate, hanging like stone icicles, the mighty stalagmites slowly building beneath them. It's a crystalline world I had never seen before. We walk on, the muffled rustle of our shoes on the cave floor, the excited comments of the tourists as we round a new curve, filling the ancient silence of the cave.

* * *

I'm broke. I have less than a dollar, but I should receive my travel pay tomorrow. It should be twenty-one dollars, so I'll be swimming in money again.

A solid rumor begins to circulate that they are going to close down the Pueblo Air Base. Only the permanent people will remain, at least for a while. They're going to have to ship us somewhere else. More rumors say we'll be divided up and sent to Lowry Field in Denver, Randolph Field in San Antonio, Alamogordo Army Airfield in New Mexico or Pyote, Texas. We hope it's not the latter as it is described as being pretty close to hell. I like Colorado and the thought of going anywhere in Texas is appalling. We may have to move out in ten days.

My parents had seen the movie, "G.I. Joe", a story about foot soldiers. They tell me that in the film, the soldiers cheered when the bombers flew over them. They want to know if that was true. I have talked with many infantry men and engineers about their reaction to our flying over them, and they say they all cheered. They said they felt sorry for us flying through all that anti-aircraft fire and were glad they weren't up there. We were glad we weren't down there slogging it out in the mud and mire.

To have so many GIs (700 of them) enrolled at Pueblo Junior College is such an unusual phenomenon that the local Pueblo newspaper covers the story. They send photographers into the classrooms to take our pictures. The Sunday edition of the paper includes a photograph of our psychology class with me in the front row.

But the situation suddenly changes. Because everyone is thrown into turmoil about the base closing and where they'll be shipped, the men are quitting their college classes. In fact, my psychology class has been disbanded. I feel sorry for the college having provided the classes and hired the teachers for us then having us bail out after only a few days. The college is getting a taste of what military life is like and may know better than to get mixed up with it again. They also have had to return all of the money we paid to sign up for the classes.

Rather than having us just sign in each day, the base commander decides to have his officers conduct drills at 0600 each morning, a decision that only adds to our discontent. It's punishment for messing up during an on-base parade, embarrassing the brass. Our confusion during the marching was the fault of our incompetent leader whose commands we couldn't hear. He's a captain and the commanding officer of our squadron, but his voice is so weak and puny that we couldn't hear his commands over the blare of band and rustle of our clodhopper shoes. I think him brainless, the most ineffective officer ever.

The following day we walk to the other side of the field for early morning drill. I'm still wearing my suntans, and the temperature is near freezing, the skies cloudy and drizzly. I shudder in the cold, adding to my disgust of the army and the unnecessary drills. After we trudge all the way out to the field, they decide to cancel the drill because of the chilly weather.

The following day we attend a big stag party in the Officers Club, the room filled with accelerating babble and good cheer. Along with others at my table I'm drinking boiler makers, beer with a shot of whisky. They're smooth and pleasant, and I'm having a good time. Explosive laughter follows sordid jokes, our table damp with spilled beer and the wet condensation from our half-filled glasses. Having had a few, I leave for the restroom. When I return and pick up my drink, it seems slightly different, but I think little of it, continuing to sip. Soon the wings of intoxication begin to take over my body, lifting me into a drunken stupor. Somehow I float to the barracks, pressure on my arms. A wild flood of words rolls out of my mouth, my friends in their bunks staring at me, perplexed. Later Keough cleans up after me with a wet mop. "It's okay Stevens," he says. I pay dearly for my indulgence, embarrassing myself before the men, the guys who had always looked up to me. It is as though I had made up for all those months of tee totaling in a single night. Only the next day, still suffering from the effects of my folly, a pounding head and a sour stomach, do I learn that when I had left for a few moments for the lavatory, my "friends" had spiked my drink with extra bourbon. I swear off boilermakers for life.

Shivering

In my thin suntan uniform, I shiver in the icy morning. It's only 0600, and a low overcast blocks what little sun is available. The Rockies are lost in clouds. We are forbidden to wear our A-2 leather flying jackets, but I get into mine on the sly sometimes to keep from turning blue. I can't wear it here on the parade ground, out in the open, where I would surely be caught.

The drill, in preparation for tomorrow's parade, seems ridiculous to me. The war is over, and many of us are on the verge of separation from the service. Why this punishment and this useless march? Is it the last chance for the commanding officers to demonstrate their power, their dominance over us?

When we begin to march, the movement will warm me up a bit. Maybe then I can stop shaking. Snow fell last night but didn't stick, the temperature outside now somewhere in the 30s.

The torture continues.

Yesterday morning we had to stand inspection, and about fifty of us hadn't received our winter clothes yet. Instead of excusing us they made us stand it anyway out there in that cold. The temperature was right around freezing, and it was awful. Everybody's faces and hands were turning blue, and most of us were shaking like leaves. The fellow in front of me was shaking so hard that I thought he would pass out. We must have stood there close to an hour. After it was over, I rolled up my sleeve, and my arm was much more blue than white. Boy, the stupidity of people around here is almost unheard of. Took me almost an hour by a stove and with hot coffee to warm up again.

My winter uniforms have not arrived from home. I need to check with the express office in town as I need them now. On the other hand there is the chance, according a flurry of rumors that we might ship out. Perhaps it will be to a place that is warmer, where we won't need them. Something else to worry about.

As I wake up the next morning and peer out the window, snow is drifting down in goose feathers. It covers the railings and a pile of stored coal, the contrast of the coal's rich black and the snow's intense white, striking. It's beautiful when we can watch it from our windows near the warmth of our thrumming pot-bellied stove. I spend a long time gazing out at the falling flakes, entranced with their motion and silence. I haven't seen it snow like this since Salt Lake City where I was stationed before being sent to Alexandria, Louisiana for training in B-17s. Gradually the falling snow becomes slushy and wet as it turns to rain, washing away the fragile blanket of white.

The following morning dawns clear and sunny, the air gradually warming up during the day. Everything is sharp and in focus, especially the Rockies powdered with new snow. It's difficult to believe how fast the weather changes here. The mountain peaks covered with new snow remind me of being home in California on a winter day following a rain when fresh snow mantles the San Gabriels, particularly Mount Baldy.

In town, I find that my winter uniforms have arrived at the Railway Express Office. My problem is that I'm going to have to send them back home.

Now comes the sad part. I had to send them right back again because we are leaving Wednesday for somewhere where they wear suntans all year round. I suppose it's Florida. I sure hate to think of going there. At least it won't be so cold.

Two Peak Moments

Sometimes I don't know what the hours will bring. Surprises materialize out of nowhere, poke through the fabric of the day, and there they are.

About noontime Keough and I decide to take in a movie in town. Scottie is kind enough to give us a ride, but as we glide along in his car he tells us that he and his wife are going to Pikes Peak. Would we like to go along? After being disappointed about missing it the last time we tried, we're excited about having another chance.

We have an hour to catch the cog train near Manitou which is fifty miles away. Scottie presses the throttle close to the floorboards. By the time we arrive and buy our tickets, we have three minutes before it leaves.

We board the Great Manitou and Pikes Peak Railway car, the train leaving just as we slide into our seats. It's jerky and slow at first, but we get used to it. The diesel engine growls and the car clanks as we ascend the steep mountain. I had hoped we would have a steam engine take us up, but it only hauls the train on the morning run. Snow patches from the recent storm still mottle the ground, adding to the spectacular views of the forests and the bare rock slopes.

At the end of the line, at the crest of Pikes Peak more snow lies in old drifts, but there is plenty of bare ground to walk around on. The view from the top is spectacular, the panorama including the plains of western Colorado, and they say, part of Kansas. Being here reminds me of flying, of riding in the nose of a B-17, looking out through that grand Plexiglas window, beholding great slices of the earth. The air is cold at 14,000 feet, but not unbearable; not as chilly as on those drill fields early in the morning. If we were flying at this altitude, we would have our oxygen masks on. As long as we walk slowly and don't exert ourselves on the mountain, we're okay. We have forty minutes to take in the view and cruise through the shops inside a rugged stone building.

I buy a delicious grilled cheese sandwich and a cup of steaming coffee at the café. It sets me back forty cents, the prices being as high as the mountain.

Two doughnuts were 15 cents. But we were starving and didn't mind the prices.

Outside again, I inhale the view. The day is so clear that it seems we can see forever. Next to California I like Colorado better than any other state, perhaps because it reminds me of California.

* * *

I had written to my parents that I might be sent to Florida the next day, but it was a ruse to set up a surprise-

--that I was actually coming home. But I can't hold back the good news.

It's only I who is going on the shipment tomorrow night. My destination is San Bernardino, California. There, within about forty-eight hours after arriving, I will be a civilian. My approval of discharge came through Saturday morning. I had to wait until Monday to clear the field…So tomorrow night at 2200 hours I'll take the Atchison, Topeka and Santa Fe for good old California. I arrive in San Bernardino at 0915 hours Saturday on the California Limited. I will report to the San Bernardino Army Air Field…I'm so happy, it's pitiful.

I had applied for a discharge several times, but at last I hit the right combination. The final approval came through in only two days. The separation of service men from all the armed forces seems to be working now.

The only sad part about leaving the service is separating from the men who had become my good friends. They hadn't had as much service time as I had, so they will be in longer. There is a good chance they will move to March Field in Riverside, close enough that I can see them once in a while. But I'm excited about my new life.

This kid is coming home for good!

Home at last, enjoying a 30-day furlough
after 34 bombing missions over Germany
and the occupied countries.

Stevens and his sister, Charline, a nurse cadet,
both home on leave in October 1944.

When away, the author longed for the peace
and security of his home. Shown are his father
and mother in their familiar dining room.

While the radar training students are relegated to
a rather desolate area called Shellbank, the rest of
Langley Field, Virginia resembles a college campus.

Stevens standing in front of his barracks in
the Shellbank section of Langley Field, ready
to begin training as a radar bombardier.

Good friends at Langley Field---
Kerley, Menke and Graef.

There were many great movies shown in the
stark Shellbank theater at Langley Field.

The plain barracks at Williams Field, Arizona are
spruced up with hardy shrubs and date palms.

Charles N. Stevens in suntan uniform at Williams Field, about to begin training on secret radar equipment.

Most of the radar training at Williams
Field is in B-24 Liberators.

Flying an observer mission near Phoenix in a B-24.

Good friends Graef, Perry and Shepherd
around the pool at Williams Field.

The "Aluminum Overcast" owned by the Experimental Aircraft Association ready to taxi at Torrance, CA in April, 2011.

The "Sentimental Journey" makes an appearance at the airfield at Gillespie Field in El Cajon, CA in June, 2011.

The "Nine-o-Nine" owned by the Collings Foundation is ready for tours at the Lyon Air Museum at John Wayne Airport in Santa Ana, CA, May, 2011.

The "Bombardier" returns to the nose of a
B-17, "Miss Angela", at the Palm Springs
Air Museum, CA in October, 2005.

The "Liberty Belle" owned by the Liberty Belle
Foundation at Bob Hope Airport in Burbank,
CA in March, 2010. (Plane tragically lost in
a fire in Aurora, Illinois on June 13, 2011)

AFTERWORD

Explanation of Additional Stories

Although the following stories do not fall within the time frame of this book, they are included because they describe incidents before or after my participation in the war or relate to me in a personal way.

"The B-17" expands on the Flying Fortress: the number made and lost as well as information about B-17s flying today.

"A Military Reunion" describes what happened at one particular gathering of the 351ˢᵗ Bomb Group in 2008, how I felt about it and the thoughts that it engendered.

"A Return to Polebrook" details a trip my wife and I made to my old field at Polebrook in England to view what was left of that once vibrant air field.

"Schweinfurt and its Ball Bearing Factories" reviews a visit to a city steeped in the lore of the 8th Air Force. Because of its key industry, the manufacturing of ball bearings, it was an important bombing target. The first raids against these plants in 1943 resulted in heavy losses for the 8th Air force. I also participated in a raid on the factories in 1944.

"Blue Fingernails" explains how I learned the effects of oxygen deprivation on my body and how that helped me on one of our combat missions.

"A Return to a B-17" concerns my visit to a B-17, "Miss Angela", at the Palm Springs Air Museum. I was allowed to get up into my old bombardier's position, which I did with great difficulty.

"The Bombing of My Hometown" depicts an incident that happened before I was in the service, on February 25, 1942. It was a night of search lights, anti-aircraft fire and "planes" over my hometown of Inglewood near Los Angeles.

"The National Archives at Suitland" deals with my visit there to search for precise information about my bombing missions. I wanted to make my book as accurate as possible, to fuse facts with my memories. It was a much more emotional experience than I thought it would be.

"An Instance at the Chickamauga Battlefield" was written after the reunion of the 351st Bomb Group in Chattanooga, Tennessee in 1996. While touring the Civil War battlefield on one of our field trips, a former airman I thought dead, boarded our bus.

"More About Hibbard's Airplane and the March of Death" portrays one incident that happened during the war and another 60 years later. Most of Hibbard's crew had bailed out over Germany in 1944. In 2008 I received a letter from James H. Harris, who had read my book, *An Innocent at Polebrook*, and informed me that he was a member of that crew. In his letters to me he describes in vivid detail what had happened to him as a prisoner of war.

"More to the Story" concerns our raid to Augsburg, Germany in 1944. Near the target we were attacked by FW-190s. Two of our planes were shot down on one pass and only two chutes were seen to open. Recently, after 67 years, I met one of those two men who had bailed out.

"Hanging around B-17s" portrays three of the remaining B-17s that fly their annual tours around the United States, some of their stops being in the Los Angeles area during the springtime. I'm there with them to answer visitors' questions about the planes and the 8th Air Force and offer my books for sale.

The B-17

Boeing B-17s served me and the rest of the 8th Air Force well during the bombing raids of World War II. Their ruggedness and effectiveness were legendary.

Between 1936 and 1945 12,731 B-17s of various models were built:

Boeing built 2,300 B-17Fs and 4,035 B-17Gs
Douglas built 605 B-17Fs and 2,395 B-17Gs
Lockheed-Vega built 500 B-17Fs and 2,250 B-17Gs

The last B-17 G was made April 9, 1945

So what happened to all those B-17s?

4,754 were either shot down, destroyed in collisions or in training accidents in the European Theater alone, approximately 3,026 in the 8th Air Force. More were lost in North Africa as well as the Pacific. Others were destroyed in crashes or had to be scrapped due to severe battle damage. Some war-torn planes became "hangar queens," good only for their parts to be used on other planes. Many were lost during training in the United States. In 1943 alone 182 B-17s crashed at the various training facilities across the United States.

Approximately 2500 B-17s that survived the war were flown by their crews back to the United States, most being stored in the Arizona desert. Row upon row of gleaming war birds covered the arid land. Almost all were scrapped.

It is a wonder that we have any B-17s left today. Only 12 B-17s are flyable in the world today. 9 are on static display in various air museums, and several others are undergoing restoration. It is a rare day that we get to see a B-17 fly.

Three B-17Gs regularly tour the United States during the spring and summer, stopping at airports throughout the country. These planes offer flights and tours and afford an excellent opportunity to approximate what it was like to fly in one of these during wartime.

Planes that make the rounds of U. S cities are the "Liberty Belle", operated by the Liberty Belle Foundation, the "Aluminum Overcast" owned by the Experimental Aircraft Association (EAA) and the "Nine-O-Nine" owned by the Collings Foundation. The latter also flies a B-24, B-25 and a P-51. Each owner has a website giving facts about the plane and a schedule of stops.

Flying in a B-17 gives a modern day person a taste of what air crews faced during World War II. Of course the flights are much shorter compared to the grueling 8-hour missions crews endured, and the altitude is low compared to the thin air at 25,000 feet where bomber crews had to use their oxygen masks. The flights are smooth and safe, and the passengers don't have to worry about encountering anti-aircraft barrages or looking out for enemy interceptors.

The plane still has great lines and poise and carries with it the mystique of all that it is famous for, the perilous bombing missions over Germany and the occupied countries that helped win World War II.

Note: Tragically on June 13, 2011, The Liberty Belle after landing safely in a corn field in Aurora, Illinois, was destroyed by a fire that had started in one engine. Fortunately none of the crew was harmed.

A Military Reunion

━━━━━━━━━

Today, in the summer of 2008, I'm flying to the Reunion of the 351st Bomb Group in Milwaukee, many thoughts tumbling around in my mind. I was a bombardier on a B-17 heavy bomber crew based at Polebrook, England in 1944. None of my crew ever attends the reunions, and I'm always apprehensive about going.

I think about my crew. I know that three of them are dead including my best friend, Jack Podoske, our co-pilot. He died some years ago on his Ohio farm when he tried to remove a stump in his front yard with a tractor that reared up and fell on him. The only other one I know that is alive is Harry Johnston, our pilot. He lives near Phoenix, Arizona where he became a bank president. He retired and played golf for years before his heart attacks. I don't know what ever happened to Warren, our navigator, Witherspoon, our radio man, or the waist gunner and ball turret man. Perhaps they are alive somewhere, but as far as I know they have faded away into obscurity. I still remember their faces and their mannerisms. I see them clearly in my imagination.

I know that Lucas, our flight engineer, died in a boating mishap rather early in his life. When in Rhode Island a number of years ago I looked up Ted Stanowick, our tail gunner. We had a good time talking about our lives and our adventures overseas while eating breakfast in a local coffee shop. I later sent him a copy of my book, but it was returned with the indication that no such person lived at that address. I stopped getting Christmas cards from him, so I assumed he had passed away.

I get a little nervous before I go to the reunions. I missed it last year, so I haven't seen any of the men for two years. I have met veterans from some of the other crews as well as their wives and now-grown "children" and have made some solid friendships over the years.

I wrote a book about my combat experiences, *An Innocent at Polebrook*, and many of the men bought copies of it, commenting favorably after they'd read it. I met more of the men this way, but perhaps they have forgotten about that after two years.

I remember the first reunion I attended, approximately ten years ago when I didn't know anyone. The men walked around with official Polebrook caps, shirts and jackets, established members of the organization. It reminded me of the way I felt when our crew first reported to Polebrook Airfield in 1944. Veterans of dangerous missions ambled around in their A-2 jackets, some decorated with the names of planes and graphics of bombs indicating how many missions they'd completed. On the walls of the officers' mess were the names of all the German and French cities the group had raided. We had yet to fly our first mission, and we were outsiders. But gradually we too became the veterans.

I was just going to have to plunge in, introduce myself and penetrate the circle. If it hadn't been for my wife Dolores who is outgoing, warm and friendly, that first reunion might have been my last. She leads the way with her congeniality and I follow in the warmth of her wake.

We're in the airport now waiting for our flight. Take off is hours away, so I have plenty of time to think about everything that's rolling around in my head.

I regret not keeping up my friendship with Jack Podoske. We were good friends and always took our leaves together, once spending a week in Scotland on what we called our flak leave. I liked him the minute I met him in Louisiana for B-17 training. I had one letter from him after coming home from overseas and then our friendship disappeared in the busyness of our lives. On our 30th mission, a difficult one to Ludwigshaven where the German gunners pummeled us with every kind of anti-aircraft gun they owned, a sharp chunk of shrapnel lodged deep in his thigh. They also knocked out part of our oxygen system, forcing us to scramble for small emergency bottles. We moved Podoske from his co-pilot seat into the nose where he could lie down. Hospitalized with his wound, he lingered in bed after his operation. I visited him several times. After completing our tour of duty, we left Polebrook, and I never saw him again. Not

ever contacting him again was a personal failure on my
part. From the letter I received from him I know that he
was dismissed from the hospital but walked gingerly on
a sore and sometimes numb leg. After I returned from
overseas I trained as a radar bombardier, was separated
from the service at war's end, attended and graduated
from UCLA and was a teacher for 32 years. In all the
energy and attention to those pursuits and the details of
everyday life, I lost touch with him. I let people go, and
they are lost to me.

Coming back to the present, I despise the indignities
of flying on commercial airliners ---the ordeal of security
checks, the long waits in the boarding areas, the cramped
quarters on the plane with its inevitable nursery of
screaming babies and fewer services.

But I love flying itself and have from the moment I
first took wing in an AT-6 at the Laredo, Texas gunnery
school. I was fascinated not only with the thrill of being
launched into the home of the clouds, but also with the
unique view of the earth, seeing it in another dimension.
Looking down on roads, the bends of the Rio Grande, the
bush-stippled hills and dry washes, villages and railroads
were new and exciting. I saw more of the earth at one time
than I had ever seen before.

Today I have a window seat on the airliner. All the
way eastward I peer down at the tapestry of our nation
that slowly drifts by beneath us. Over the hazy grays and
beiges of the desert, I look down on bone-dry washes,
powdery dry lakes and sharp arid ranges. Dirt roads, like

nerves, run through them, and modern highways and railroads cut lonely paths. The blue ribbon of the Colorado River tells us we are leaving California. We jet through the thin air at 39,000 feet, yet towering thunderheads reach our altitude, our pilot avoiding those menacing castles. The Rockies rise beneath us, their bare tops above the timberline still dappled with patches of snow. The dry plains pass under us, the green circles of irrigated crops appearing like great domino dots on the face of the land. We come upon the patchwork of the Middle West, an unending quilt of rectangular plots---green, tan, yellow, earth color---the gray-blue shadows of clouds playing over them. Nestled among the fields are the grids of small towns. Interstate highways insinuate themselves over the land with the pleasing geometry of their on and off ramps.

I can't help but think of the contrast between flying now and flying our missions back in 1944. Here we are flying 14,000 feet higher than we ever flew on our bombing raids, yet despite the thin freezing air outside, we ride in comfort. We relax in our cushioned chairs and have no trouble breathing, the temperature as perfect as in our living room at home. I remember how cold it was on our missions, my heated suit barely adequate, my chair a little stool, breathing in oxygen through my mask, burdened with equipment and apprehensions.

I nearly doze in my luxurious surroundings as we near Milwaukee, but again I think about Jack Podoske. Several years ago we visited Jack's widow who still lives in their Ohio home, not far from Columbus. She is a petite woman with a soft voice, her gray hair pulled back. She is still very much in love with Jack, and talks about him with nearly every breath. She lives by herself except for a Doberman and a husky police dog that watch over her. As she has always done, she cans fruits and vegetables, especially tomatoes and string beans that she grows in her garden. A large color portrait of Jack in his officer's uniform rests on a table in the living room. I meet Jack's two daughters, one of whom resembles her father. I am introduced to their husbands and children as well. I think about how much Jack would have enjoyed being with them.

My ears respond to our letting down into the Milwaukee area, our plane banking in a wide turn over Lake Michigan, ducking in and out of clouds. On the approach we fly low over industrial buildings, a railroad and parked cars, touching down smoothly. The grass at the airport is as green as Ireland.

A shuttle van whisks us to our hotel. After storing our bags in our room, we walk down to the hospitality room, where the members meet to talk, look at memorabilia, consume free drinks and nibble on goodies. This is when the butterflies begin to flutter, their soft wings tickling my belly. Even before we reach the room, chatter and laughter spill out of the doorway. We register then turn to the makeshift bar, a table bearing ranks of liquor and soft drink bottles. A woman I had met at a previous reunion gives me a good hug, the softness of her cheek as well as her kind words about my book, instantly dissolving my apprehensions. A woman behind the table pours gin over ice cubes for me. I sip it slowly, the plastic cup cold, my spirits warming. I see some men I know and a few I don't know, and there are handshakes, some firm and some soft. Like me, many of the vets are showing their age, a few with canes or walkers, others with wheel chairs or scooters. Many, like me, still walk unassisted, albeit a trifle slower than in former years. I'm surprised that some of the vet's sons appear to be as old as their fathers. Several men remark favorably about my book and remember me, further allaying my tensions. I introduce myself to those who don't know me while Dolores sails up to people and talks to them as though she has known them all of her life, a talent I don't have.

Back in the hospitality room once again, I sit with a glass of white wine and a stack of ten of my books. I sell them all in short order, making new friends in the process. I feel honored that people like and buy my book, and I enjoy meeting these people.

The vets and some of their family members sit around the tables renewing acquaintances, thumbing through old photo albums of our base at Polebrook and talking over old times while they sip drinks.

One of our bus trips takes most of us to the Air Museum at Oshkosh, about an hour and a half from Milwaukee. The journey itself is relaxing as we roll over the landscape of rural Wisconsin. We roll by white farm houses set far back off the road, silver silos and wooden Scandinavian barns set on rock foundations. Long leaves of foot-high corn, rustle in the breeze. Wild flowers push up among grasses and healthy trees congregate into dark green forests.

The EAA Air Museum is first rate, and we all enjoy viewing the shiny meticulously restored aircraft on display. We are all together doing the same thing, walking and looking yet being with each other.

Later at the group's buffet dinner we sit with people we know, the conversation free-flowing and comfortable. One man at the table is 93 years old and one of the original cadre of the 351st Bomb Group. A dignified man in a dark suit, he is still crowned with pure white wavy hair and penetrating eyes.

We arrive rather late at the banquet the following day, the culmination of our reunion. The men look nice in their suits and the women in their fine dresses. We sit at a table we had signed up for, but only one other couple is at the table, the rest of the chairs empty. Finally four more people arrive at our table and conversation bubbles.

The highlight of the evening is the taking of a group photograph of the veteran airmen. Out of 120 people at the reunion only 30 of us are vets, the rest of them being wives, offspring and grandchildren, even cousins. We have our picture taken officially and by almost everyone else, the cameras flashing like a violent electrical storm.

I can't help but contrast this tableau with an imaginary one taken over sixty years ago of the same group of veterans---when we were young, vigorous, virile and had our whole lives to look forward to.

At a meeting earlier in the day our chaplain read off the list of those who had died since our last reunion. There were 90 names, the passing of the veterans accelerating at a rapid rate. Our leader is 88 years old and is beginning to become more frail. He leads us in the Air Corps song, his high pitched foggy voice belting the words out as best he can. I've forgotten some of the words so I mumble a few and wait until the lines are familiar.

In our hospitality room I'm not hearing as many war stories since over sixty years later they've all been told a number of times. The conversations are more about illnesses, old age and people they used to know. With many people attending who have never been in combat, it is natural for topics to turn to everyday affairs.

All of us vets are in our 80s and 90s, some in respectable shape for our ages, but some not. Most of us wear glasses and hearing aids, sometimes necessitating the asking of questions two or three times before getting an answer. But there is a definite camaraderie among men who have all been through the same ordeals--- have flown through flak barrages, endured fighter attacks, suffered with the cold at high altitude, endured the burden of heavy and binding flying clothes---flak suits, parachute harnesses, Mae Wests, intercom wires and oxygen masks---but most of all, we had looked death in the eye and stood our ground.

I know that some of the men had more harrowing experiences than I did, some perhaps less, but we all endured our missions, went through the tensions of briefing and debriefing, yearned for home and family and looked forward to mail call every day.

Reunions always make me think about age, my age. How much time do I have left? How many men attending this reunion will never be at another? When I read in the paper that certain projects I am interested in will be completed in 2015 or 2018, I'm always concerned that I might not be around when they are completed. I suppose this is natural for a man my age. But I don't worry about it, don't let it damage the quality of my life now. I love my life and look forward each day to all that lies ahead. I am in reasonably good health, financially comfortable, happily married and I am blessed with family and friends.

We are zooming out west now at high altitude, the land passing beneath us like a slowly unrolling scroll. Bits of the reunion still dance in my head. The life blood of our 351st Bomb Group Organization lies in the sons and daughters and their progeny. They possess the energy to keep the association going. They still revere their fathers for the men they are and what they did so long ago. Some still attend even though their fathers have passed away.

When all of the vets are gone, will the association still be alive? Perhaps I will be the last vet to attend.

Note: At Christmas time 2010 I received a card from Maxine Johnston, wife of my pilot, Harry Johnston which said : "Just a short note to let you know. Harry passed away in October 2009. I really miss that wonderful man."

A Return to Polebrook

In 1998 Kings Cross Station appears much as I remember it from our leaves to London in 1944, a cavernous place with a huge curving glass skylight. Although modernized, many of the old arched steel beams still support the roof. Fifty-four years ago a palpable haze hovered over the tracks, the smoke and vapors from the clanking steam locomotives. Today the air is much clearer.

Our train for Peterborough leaves on time, snaking out of the station with its string of sleek modern coaches, dark blue with a persimmon stripe down the center. Our locomotive today is a powerful diesel as streamlined as a .50 caliber bullet.

We roll smoothly by the same old clutter along the tracks, the smoke-stained bridges and short black tunnels that I remember from so many years ago.

Once out in the countryside, we streak past green fields and hills, splashing streams and placid canals, at speeds only imagined in 1944. Our slower trips of those days were in the summer when the trees had all leafed out, adding their richness to the verdant pastures. Now, in March, many trees still stand winter-bare, a few of them just beginning to bud, their branches sleeved softly in green, the white popcorn-like blossoms of blackthorn promising spring.

I remember how comforting it was to look out of the train windows at the pastoral fields and the peaceful beauty of the land, the farms and grazing sheep, as an antidote for the grim business of flying bombing missions. Gazing on them now brings back some of those same feelings.

New housing covers much of the former open areas, especially around Peterborough where recently-built tracts ring the old town. The sharp spires of the Cathedral still point heavenward, however, like a focal point in the center of the city. Instead of the two-hour trip that I remember, we arrive in Peterborough in only 40 minutes.

Waiting at the station for us is Dave Gower, tall, dressed in jeans and a flannel shirt, his gray-streaked hair ruffled by the wind. After a cheerful greeting we walk to his Land Rover and are soon on our way to Polebrook over a modern dual carriageway, a contrast to the ribbon-like road that existed before.

On the outskirts of Polebrook Airfield we turn at a narrow road leading toward the area where we once walked through the woods to the movie theater. We pause at the rutted dirt path, much of it muddy, most of the trees naked, the chestnuts just beginning to unfurl their first leaves. I remember the tree-dappled shade of summer there. I had always liked walking among the trees, feeling that for a few moments I was out of the war, seeing nothing above but the fragments of blue sky through the trees.

We peek into the old Red Cross building, now decaying, the glass from the window panes all broken out, portions of the brick wall caved in. Locals still store some battered-looking farm equipment inside.

The building nearby where we used to enjoy American movies is also decrepit, a wood cutting operation with machinery at one end. Pale painted figures, so faded as to be barely discernable, remain on one wall---one a well-endowed woman, the other a sweating musician playing the drums. Imagining ourselves once watching movies in this relic is quite difficult. The films were very important to us then, as they took our minds off the war for a few hours, and transported us back to theaters in our hometowns.

Entering the airfield itself, we pass through what used to be the main gate. We then turn down a narrow road, now crowded with small trees and shrubs at its edge, that formerly led to our barracks and the officer's mess hall. Where our barracks once stood, grasses, bushes and tangles of brambles now reign. The cold sterile overgrown brush was a startling contrast to the warmth and vitality that once occurred here---active young bodies and voices, fears and apprehensions, homesickness, laughter and horseplay, camaraderie, our leaving the doors in the dark for missions, our return buoyant with the euphoria of having survived another raid, our sorrows about those who did not come back.

When visiting old ruins, Roman, Greek or medieval, I have often thought about the humanity that once dwelled there, have tried to imagine what life was like for them. Now I find it strange that I myself was part of the humanity that once was part of these more modern ruins, these naked foundations now reclaimed by wild vegetation.

Dave drives us out to see the triangular granite monument commemorating the record of the 351st Bomb Group, a magnificent tribute to all men who flew from Polebrook. The well-tended stone stands in a grassy area flanked by poplar trees, all of which rest on a small preserved section of the old runway. On it are the following words:

The 351st Bomb Group at Polebrook
operated in England from 1943 to 1945.
They flew 311 combat missions.
175 B-17s and their crews were lost. They
shot down 303 enemy fighters.

The entire expanse that the runway once occupied is still open space, the only impediments stacks of baled hay scattered about like geometric blocks. Natural grasses cover the field, now mown only once per year. As we ride along a road paralleling the ghost of the runway, a pheasant flies out of the grass, and dozens of white-tailed rabbits hop near one of the old air raid shelters. Across the field stands the last remaining hangar with its great curved roof.

Although the monument is very meaningful to me, the remaining patch of asphalt runway stimulates my imagination even more. I walk around on the very stuff from which we took off---our plane revving, shuddering then letting go, lumbering down the runway burdened with bombs and fuel.

We visit Dave Gower's offices in the old hanger, its enormous interior now filled with tons of wheat rather than B-17s. His modern quarters contain the desks, files and computers necessary for his business. I sign the guest book, adding my name to the many other men who have returned to Polebrook for one last look.

On the train back to London I realize what revisiting Polebrook has meant to me. I had written much about the war to pass on to the family who came after me, the task relieving my mind of much that had lodged there, but had never been expressed. Putting it all down on paper had been cathartic. Somehow I had felt more at ease. The trip back to Polebrook seemed a final act of closure for that long ago turbulent time.

Note: My respectful thanks to Dave Gower who gave up time from his busy schedule to pick us up and return us to Peterborough, show us the remains of Polebrook Field, take us to an old pub for lunch and generally treat us royally.

Schweinfurt and Its Ball Bearing Factories

━━━━━━━

During the Second World War two of the greatest air battles were fought during raids directed at the ball bearing plants just outside of Schweinfurt, Germany. The attacks occurred in August and October 1943, both sides sustaining heavy losses. The 8th Air Force lost 60 heavy bombers on the first try and 60 on the second as well as losing many other planes that were so badly damaged that they crashed back in England or had to be scrapped. Our losses were so devastating that unescorted daylight raids deep into Germany were suspended. The word "Schweinfurt" took on a kind of mystique, a symbol for horror and defeat for airmen. In 1944 I participated in a raid on Schweinfurt as the bombed ball bearing factories were again operating and were vital to the German war machine. With its reputation as a difficult target, one might imagine what was going through my mind. But this time we were protected by American fighter planes and survived the raid with no losses to our group.

On a river cruise in 2005, one of our stops was at Schweinfurt. Because of the city's symbolic nature in 8th Air Force lore, I especially wanted to visit it. Nearing the town on the Main River, we pass one of the huge SKF roller bearing plants still operating, a modern industrial building that rose out of the ashes of war.

The weather had been threatening all morning, and now, just as we reach Schweinfurt, the rain begins to fall. As we dine on chicken and spaghetti Bolognese in the ship's warm, comfortable dining room we watch the town disappear in mist through our rain-streaked windows.

By mid afternoon the rain stops, and we begin our walking tour of the town. We first enter the large market square, pausing in front of the spectacular Rathaus, or city hall, a tall gothic structure built in 1570 and still displaying the Hapsburg eagle. Nearby stands a statue of Friedrick Rucker who died in 1866 and was said to speak 44 languages and compose 20,000 poems, some of which were set to music by Mahler and Brahms.

Today 55,000 people live in Schweinfurt, most of them employed in the roller bearing plants. The vast market square, Martin Luther Platz, appears to be the hub of activity in the town. Narrow side streets lead off of it. From the modern look of the buildings around it I imagine that some of the original ones were damaged in the war. Whatever was battered or destroyed in air raids then is now rebuilt. Commerce is lively. People walk in and out of wine shops displaying gleaming bottles from the local vineyards, stroll into bakeries with many varieties of golden-crusted breads temptingly lying on racks in the windows, and shop in clean delicatessens burgeoning with abundance. There are drug stores, beauty shops and boutiques that one might find in any vital city.

The people here are like people everywhere. School kids skip along with their backpacks. Teenagers look like teenagers, some with rings in their lips, ears and nose. Matronly women shop for groceries, and a few old men walk with canes. Pretty young women are in full flower; a few assuming a rebellious look with their dangling cigarettes.

Off Martin Luther Platz we enter St. Johannes Church, built in the 13th century. It seems rather ordinary to us except for its magnificent baroque pulpit, its carved wood gilded and gleaming. The church was nearly destroyed by an air raid in 1944, then carefully restored to its original appearance.

We visit three museums, all of which are free. The Altes Gymnasium Museum displays some of the very old drawings of Schweinfurt complete with its fortifications and medieval city walls. There are also paintings of the town before World War II. Nowhere in any of the museums is there a photograph or drawing of any building damaged by the war. It is as though the war didn't happen, that there is only Schweinfurt before the war and modern Schweinfurt.

Another shower sweeps the square as we head back to the ship. Holding our umbrellas as steady as we can in the wind, we try to fend it off. Closer to the river we visit their cold, dank natural history museum housing glass cases of stuffed birds.

It is warm and pleasant back on the ship. We dine on halibut and smoked salmon, quiche and vegetarian dishes then finish with apple pie.

I discover that one of the women in our group of travelers was born in Schweinfurt and still has relatives that live in the area. She was a young girl during the war and often had to scurry to the shelters during air raids. At her tender age, she thought the bombing raids were nuisances that interrupted play. When she swam in a nearby quarry she had to find shelter among the rocks when there were air raid warnings. When I participated in the bombing raid on Schweinfurt she was a blond-haired five-year-old scrambling for the shelters with her family. Since we flew at such a high altitude people on the ground were invisible to us, so the war seemed rather impersonal. As I talk to this woman (now an American citizen), a little girl who was down there on July 21, 1944 when we flew over at 25,000 feet and dropped our load of 500-pound bombs on the ball bearing factories, the war becomes more personal to me.

At night the bars and discos of the town are in full swing, the lights blinking, the music thudding through the streets. The golden arches of McDonald's shine brightly in the darkness.

Blue Fingernails

The huge metal tank looks like a miniature submarine, and we are about to board it. I am at Ellington Field in 1943 for bombardier pre flight training, and the giant tank is a pressure chamber. Nine of us enter it through a small steel door and take our places at small tables, oxygen masks and flexible tubing at each one of them. The operators are going to lower the pressure inside to simulate conditions at high altitude.

We had heard rumors (there were always rumors) that several cadets had been hospitalized as a result of these tests, and that others who were claustrophobic had beaten on the door with their fists and begged to be let out. There was always something to raise our tensions.

At last the men in charge close the door then tighten it for a perfect seal. A port hole in the door allows them to observe us. At first the pressure is lowered to simulate 5,000 feet. They ask us to clear our ears by yawning, swallowing and working ours jaws like cows chewing their cud. Three cadets can't clear their ears and are let out of the tank.

With our oxygen masks in place we are taken up to 35,000 feet. The difference in pressure inside and outside our bodies causes pressure/volume exchanges within us. We burp behind our masks and pass gas frequently. There is no room for modesty in the pressure chamber. One cadet suddenly leans forward in pain and yells that he has the bends. The sergeant outside tells him over a speaker system that it's just trapped gas and that he should just hang on.

After bringing us back down, the operator tells us that he's going to take us up to over 30,000 feet, but we are not to apply our oxygen masks until we feel about to pass out. He tells us that each person will experience different symptoms when deprived of oxygen, and we are to determine what our specific symptoms are.

Most of the cadets, feeling light headed, slap on their masks just before we get to 20,000 feet. I wait a little longer, but begin to get woozy. What I notice more than anything is that my fingernails have turned blue---my tell-tale symptom of anoxia. A few deep breaths from my oxygen mask restore me.

* * *

On September 8, 1944 we are on our 30th mission, a raid on the I.G.Farben Chemical Works at Ludwigshaven, Germany. Anti-aircraft fire on the bomb run is unusually brutal. The German gunners are firing everything they have at us, 88s as well as 105s, the flak bursts black, but with white ones tinted with pink among them. We are all taking hits, but our four engines churn through the icy, shrapnel-saturated air.

Suddenly our pilot, Harry Johnston, informs us that our co-pilot, Jack Podoske, has been hit. The flight engineer and navigator grab emergency oxygen bottles and move him down into the nose where he can lie down. His flying suit is ripped and bloody. He's taken a large hunk of flak on the inside of his thigh.

I notice that I'm beginning to feel light headed. I rip off one glove and see that my fingernails have turned blue, just as they were in that pressure chamber so many months before. Since flak had damaged part of our oxygen system, I switched to an emergency oxygen bottle and soon felt much better,

Once we are on our way home and over the portion of France liberated by our troops, our whole group lowers altitude, so low we don't need the oxygen masks. We zoom over France nearly on the deck, the surprised French farmers waving at us as we roar over. Bearing up well with his injury, Podoske will soon be back at Polebrook and be attended to at the base hospital.

And I'm glad I found out about blue fingernails.

A Bombardier Returns to a B-17

"Why don't you go on up," says the guide at the Palm Springs Air Museum. "Get up there in the nose and sit in your old bombardier's seat." I hadn't been in that seat for over 60 years.

I walk through the shadow beneath the great wing of the B-17 bomber, "Miss Angela", approaching the metal ladder leading up and into the escape hatch under the nose.

My God, I think. When I was 19 I used to grab the edge of the hatch, pull myself up then throw my legs inside. I couldn't even pull myself up now. Thank goodness for the ladder.

I step gingerly up its rungs, holding on to the slim handrails. When I reach the top I inhale that familiar airplane smell of metal, oil and plastic.

I crawl off the top steps, entering on my knees into the compartment, guarding my head from the low ceiling. The plane had been standing out in the sun all day, and it's hot inside, like one of those sun ovens they use in India. It is so unlike the missions we had flown in the freezing temperatures of high altitude.

Well, I can't skitter into the bombardier's compartment like I used to. That's for sure. I sit for a moment trying to compose myself, trying to figure out how I'd move through. I'd grab something, anything, then pull myself along. I progress slowly at first, grasping some netting which soon gives way. My limbs feel as though they're packed with lead shot. I get around more like a hippopotamus than a bombardier. How was it before? It had been so easy, so routine to enter here. I never had to think about it. But I was 19 and weighed only 140 pounds then. Now here I am on the floor contemplating my next move.

I shuffle on my knees through the navigator's compartment, past the little table and the whisker machine guns, the place where Warren, our navigator, used to spread out his maps and keep track of our position. With what energy I have left, I scoot toward the bombardier's seat, towards that place that holds so many memories --- the beauty of clouds, of hills, rivers and towns far below, the nightmare of anti-aircraft barrages and wounded planes. I had seen so much from that Plexiglas fishbowl. Finally, with more space above my head, I pull myself up to a standing position. I sit down in the old swivel seat, a dusty Norden bombsight in front of me. I look at it, trying to remember which dials I used to turn-- which for range and which for drift? It had been so many years ago, and the automatic moves ingrained in me during bombardier training at Midland, Texas had disappeared from my memory. I hadn't touched one in over 60 years, not since crew training in Alexandria, Louisiana in 1944. I never used one overseas.

Down below on the ramp my wife and the guide look up at me. If they only knew how frustrated I had been just trying to reach that seat! They both want me to pose for pictures of the old bombardier returning to his position. I look down and try to smile.

"Hey," yells the guide. "When you're finished there, you can go back through the bomb bays then out the side door."

I wallow back through the navigator's space to the area beneath the cockpit. I sit there wondering how the hell I'm going to crawl up through that small opening. I finally decide to pull myself up, grasping any surface I can find. I struggle to my feet and stand looking at the myriad dials, gauges and switches on the dash of the pilot's compartment. This is where our pilot Johnston sat and beside him Podoske, our co-pilot.

Ducking my head, I pass through the tight quarters of the top turret, stumbling over the mechanism on the floor, the place where Lucas, the flight engineer, used to stand and watch the instruments. Before me is the bomb bay, its doors open, the concrete ramp visible below. Most of the bomb racks had been removed, leaving just two with dummy bombs attached. My God, the catwalk through the bomb bay is narrow! Was it always that narrow? And the metal struts supporting it. They're so close together! It would be tight, pushing my body through that narrow space. I carefully step down onto the catwalk, placing one foot in front of the other. The dimensions are snug when I squeeze through the struts, my soft belly slithering past the hard metal.

Okay, I've made it. I step into the light of the radio room, some of the old scratched and dusty radio equipment still anchored to the wall. I remember our radioman, Witherspoon, having problems with airsickness. I walk on past the ball turret where Caruso's body had been riddled with flak on our mission to Hamburg. I move into the waist, the exposed interior like the ribs of a whale. I stand poised at the small ladder at the waist door.

"If I were you, I'd go down that ladder backwards. It's easier and safer," says the guide.

I comply and soon feel the sun-warmed concrete beneath my feet. I walk out past the wing then look back at the old bomber gleaming in the desert afternoon. I had always admired its lines, and it still looks good to me. It is magnificent, poised on the apron in front of the hangar, its sleek aluminum body dazzling. There is something about that long tapering fin on top of the fuselage that leads to the tail. It is so distinctive and pleasing to the eye.

Two mechanics work on the right outboard engine, one starting it in the cockpit while the other observes from the outside. The engine whines and coughs into life, a pulsing rhythm of powerful pistons and a wisp of blue smoke. How familiar that sound is.

It's all very romantic. The B-17 is associated with a pivotal part of my life. I learned then that I could face danger, even the possibility of my own death, and not shirk from it. I could perform my duties even though I was apprehensive and fearful when flying through flak barrages and worried about possible fighter attacks.

Here I am on a benign sunny afternoon in Palm Springs, an 80 year-old man remembering his past, but living very much in the present. The experience of going through the ancient Flying Fortress had told me much about myself, how I was then and how I am now.

I walk toward my wife, slip my arm around her and look westward toward the sharp San Jacinto Mountains, clouds resting on their higher peaks.

The Bombing of My Hometown

===================

Anti-aircraft shells burst like sinister orange blossoms where the searchlight beams converge in the cold February night in 1942. Other than the intense blue of the probing lights, only the stars add their feeble glow to the darkness. Blackout curtains block out any stray rays from the houses, and the streetlights had been darkened soon after the air raid siren sounded its melancholy wailing. What I behold is totally alien to the quiet peace of my hometown, Inglewood, California. I wonder uneasily whether the enemy aircraft caught in the spokes of the beams might drift directly over our neighborhood or whether they might spare us, concentrating instead on the oil refineries or the aircraft factories. I shiver with excitement during my short trip down the driveway from my bed in the garage to the house. I had no idea that the sounds that had intruded into my sleep would sweep me into such turbulence or lead in the end to such surprises.

The cold night air, smelling faintly of dew on dust and

plants, numbs my nose and creeps under my robe, sending a shudder through my already tense body. The anti-aircraft fire thuds in the heavens like concussion bombs on the Fourth of July. Somewhere in the blackness the air raid warden wearing his hard hat walks the streets looking for errant lights from houses. The avocado tree next to the driveway where we stand rustles in a whisper of wind.

Only a few moments before, my father had opened the garage door, the small wheel that supported it rolling and grinding on the concrete driveway.

"Get up Norman!" he shouted urgently, his voice higher than normal, "We're having an air raid! You better come in the house!"

As a high school student, I had been sleeping in the garage inside of a special study room that my father and I built together. Now, my father, fearing for my safety, had come to fetch me. Although the house was no safer, he wanted us to be together.

The explosions had wakened me earlier. I lay back on my pillow in the darkness with my eyes wide as teacups. I then sat up in bed, peering out of the small window that faced the neighbor's yard. Only the night before, a Japanese submarine surfaced in the inky waters just north of Santa Barbara, lobbing several shells into a cluster of oil storage tanks. I decided that several enemy subs must have been shelling the Standard Oil refinery at El Segundo. In my imagination I saw the shells exploding among the cracking towers and the camouflaged tanks. Hearing my father's pleas, I grab my robe and fumble in the gloom for my slippers. We both pause in the driveway, glancing one last time at the sky before we enter the house. The high-flying enemy aircraft, caught in the web of lights, their underbellies specks of fluorescent blue, speed off toward the north, the beams moving with them, the flame-orange anti-aircraft bursts popping in their midst. My father and I stare at the sky with a strange fascination, a blend of terror and curiosity.

In the house my mother runs water full force into the bathtub, a precaution in case our water supply should be cut off. The sound of the rushing water fills the dark house. My father cracks open one window, peering out through the screen for the next wave of bombers. His hands, lips and body tremble in the dull light. I have never seen him like this before. Our dim forms flutter in the dark room. I consider the possibility of my life being snuffed out by a stray bomb, and I know that the same thought disturbs my father. I envision the wreckage of the factories where our neighbors work and even the destruction of Market Street, the main boulevard of our town, where we shopped and where I had whistled in the theaters when the afternoon matinees began.

After a lull, the thudding of the anti-aircraft fire renews, this time to the south. Suddenly the enemy aircraft release their bombs, a quick volley of thundering explosions that briefly light up the sky and flicker through the cracked-open window. The blasts erupt from the direction of the airport where the North American Aircraft factory must have taken a direct hit. I imagine the sleek Mustang fighter planes lined up outside the factory, a torn and tangled junkyard of twisted aluminum.

The attack we had expected, the one that the military forces had prepared for the last several months had at last happened.

The attack apparently over, the enemy planes head out to sea in the dying night. Still agitated, my mind seething with frightening images, I return to my room in the garage for a few final hours of sleep. I think again about our peaceful street where I had grown up with the other children my age, where the only violence had been a sporadic sharp word or a short-lived argument about who had been shot first in a game of cops and robbers.

I listen with disbelief to the radio reports as broadcasting resumes in the morning. The newscasters declare emphatically, that although something may have been overhead during the night, they could not confirm that they had been enemy aircraft. They further state that no bombs had been dropped, no damage had been done and no planes had been shot down.

"They're crazy!" I shout as I stalk across the living room floor in my slippers. "They're not telling the truth! What's the matter with them!"

I had heard the awful thunder of the bombs from the direction of the airport, and I had clearly seen the enemy planes snared in the searchlights. I assume that the news is being altered as a cover-up, a distortion to confuse the enemy. The defense forces offer no explanation, maintaining silence in the name of wartime secrecy. I am impatient with the newscasts. Not only are they withholding the truth, but they also challenge my personal integrity, my perceptions and my sense of reality. They steal away the tension and drama of my experience. I had survived the first Japanese air attack on the continental United States. I had witnessed the terror of falling bombs, the spectacle of alien planes and the valiant efforts of our own armed forces as they courageously fought off the invaders with withering anti-aircraft fire.

The high school campus next day buzzes with rumors. "They were Japanese planes, and I know one of them was shot down," says one of my friends. "It crashed near a gasoline station, and my uncle saw the insignia. They roped off the street and wouldn't let anyone through. They hauled the plane away so nobody could find out about it." Another boy speaks up, "The planes were really our own. A squadron of Navy planes flew in from San Francisco without the right identification, so they shot at them. The gunners were so bad they couldn't hit any of them." Still another joined in, "I heard it was really the Goodyear blimp."

The evening newspapers restrain themselves by making no definite statements, leaving doubts that any enemy airplanes had flown over the night before. I have to admit to myself that since the airport and all of its facilities remain intact, the concussions I had assumed to be falling bombs must have actually been the rapid firing from a battery of anti-aircraft guns.

The newspapers intimate that the firing may have arisen out of confusion, a lack of communication or mass hysteria. This may very well be, but I clearly saw those airplanes winging silently over the city, their distant undersides a ghostly silver-blue in the converging shafts of light. At least I think I did.

The National Archives at Suitland

On a special green sheet, I made a request for the records of the first three missions I had flown over fifty years ago.

"351st Heavy Bombardment Group"
"Le Bourget, France June 14,1944"
"Angouleme, France June 15, 1944"
"Hamburg, Germany June 18, 1944"

I wait in a cold room at the National Archives in Suitland, Maryland for one of the clerks to locate the files, and bring them to me. It should take him at least one-half hour. I look down the rows of tables lit by the pale gloom seeping in through the windows from the cloudy skies outside. Shelves of books run along the walls, and several copying machines stand on the other side of the room near the windows. I'm here to research the bombing missions I flew from Polebrook, England, hoping to blend the facts from the records with my memories so that the book I am writing will be accurate and detailed.

The woman standing at the small reception desk near the door asked me to sign in, and fill out papers for a special researcher's card. Another woman at the desk, a heavy woman wearing a bright blue dress and glasses, had given me instructions through her thick Southern accent. Talking confidently and forcefully from her vast experience on the job, she told me exactly what to do. She graciously explained how to fill out the forms for the records that I had requested. Neither woman had been born when the records I wanted were written.

Glad I had kept my sweater on in the chilly room, I run my fingers over the spines of the old books on the shelves, thinking I might find some useful information about my bombing group or the war in general, but I find nothing pertinent. The musty smell of the books and the linoleum floor remind me of being in our Inglewood Library when I was a kid.

Finally the young man brings me two pressboard filing boxes containing the records. The boxes feel cold in my hands, as though they had been stored in a refrigerated room. I place them carefully on the table, folding back the top of one of them on its paper hinges. The stiff white folders stand in the box, their tabs hand written. Scrawled across the tab of the second folder are the words, "Le Bourget, Mission #154, June 14, 1944". As I reach for the folder, my body trembles, perhaps enhanced by the chill that pervades the room. I feel as though the energy of that time again courses through my body like a weak electrical charge, my reaction more visceral than I thought it would be.

I open the folder, fingering through its yellowing reports with their frayed edges and fading print. The papers, folded for years into permanent creases, with their crude typing and ink stains, represent all the facts of my first mission. The facts and statistics lie pressed in the folder I hold in my hands, but this is not <u>my</u> personal folder that holds the bowel-churning excitement, numbing fear, wild apprehensions, nightmarish sights, acute discomfort and bone-chilling cold of the mission. It is like a flat sketch without depth, without dimensions. Only I can flesh out the facts on the tattered papers before me. Only I can add the dimensions that still lie along my nerves, rest in the deep folds of my mind, and hide in the shadows of my memory.

I handle the old papers with care, letting half-century-old memories rush back and have their way. I jot down notes and take fragile papers to the copying machine, remind myself about bomb loads, times, altitudes, weather, and targets, the facts themselves often triggering other recollections. I piece it all together, fly the mission again, and dig deep into my own history.

An Instance at the
Chickamauga Battlefield

━━━━━━━━

Our bus rolls through the park-like site of the Chickamauga Battlefield in 1996 at Chattanooga, Tennessee. We are veterans of World War II, airmen of the 351st Bomb Group, looking out on the monuments to the dead of another war. The Civil War was just one of many wars that occur with regularity, sweeping like a consuming tide of blood over the land, stealing lives away from young men, robbing them of their potential and all that might have been. The names of these Civil War dead are carved in granite and embossed on the brass plaques of state monuments scattered around the military park. We of the 351st Bomb Group also have a monument, on the grassy outskirts of Polebrook, a small town in England. Statistics are inscribed on its polished granite surface, but none of the names of those who died in our 175 bombers shot down are carved in the stone. But the men are just as dead.

After stopping at a monument, we return to our bus. Sitting near the front, I watch the men and their wives boarding the bus, casually reading their name tags as they file slowly down the aisle. As one of the name tags floats by me, I gasp. I recognize the name "Dixey" as a pilot whose plane had been shot down on my first mission in 1944, to Le Bourget Airfield near Paris. I had seen a plane explode in a blinding yellow blast that had reminded me of a gigantic dandelion flower. I had neither known the man at the time nor heard of his name. I had known only that one of our planes had been hit by anti-aircraft fire, and exploded. The plane still explodes in my mind, has exploded there again and again. Only one year ago I pored through the mission reports of our group in the National Archives, taking notes for future writing. The mission report stated, "Aircraft 42-97066, Pilot Lt. Dixey, was lost just after bombs away when accurate flak was encountered. The aircraft blew up as a result of a direct hit by flak." Dixey was a rare name, and it had stuck in my mind. It would be unusual to have two people with such a name in the same group. My curiosity aroused, I plan to talk to him about it at the first opportunity.

After stopping at the Chickamauga Battlefield Monument where we all get off the bus again, I manage to catch up to him. Sidling up to him in the shadow of the monument, I say, "Pardon me. Were you a pilot with our group?" Somewhat surprised at my question, he answers, "Yes, I was." My next question is about his being shot down. Again he answers, "Yes, I was. I was shot down on my twenty-fourth mission, to Le Bourget."

Still perplexed, I say, "But according to the mission report your plane blew up when you were hit with flak. I saw it explode. There was no mention of parachutes." He says, "Well, it wasn't quite like that. Our plane was on fire. I had trouble keeping the plane level because the left wing wanted to dip. I told everyone to bail out while I held the plane as steady as I could. I sent the engineer back to check that everyone was out of the plane before I let go of the controls. He returned quickly, and said that everyone was out, then he jumped. I got behind the pilot's seat to snap on my chest pack. With the plane burning and now twisting into a violent left-hand spin I ended up in the nose section. I received a nasty blow on the head, but remained conscious as I fought my way to the escape hatch. I hesitated a moment because the angle of the plane and the way it was spinning seemed to put me on a path with the left inboard propeller. I jumped anyway, and thank God I missed it. Soon after I got out, the plane exploded."

His parachute came down near Paris, but luckily he was intercepted by the French Underground who hid him for ten weeks before the Allied troops entered the area.

Shortly after we talk, Dixey introduces his wife, Jane, to Dolores and me. She tells us that they were engaged at the time he was shot down, that she heard nothing except that he was missing in action for over ten weeks. Finally word came through that he was reported "alive and well". They were married after his return home, and recently celebrated their 50th wedding anniversary.

Later, at our reunion banquet, we see them on the

dance floor as we waltz by. They smile at us, and say hello. They are a handsome couple. He is quiet but dignified, she outgoing and lively, a dazzling light in her eyes. I thought that this man, a man I had not known except for his name, could have been a name inscribed into some war memorial, like the names we had seen on the monuments in the Chickamauga Battlefield. For some reason it fills me with great pleasure to see him dancing now with his attractive wife.

More about Hibbard's Airplane and the March of Death

———

In *An Innocent at Polebrook* I wrote a chapter titled "Hibbard's Airplane," which is an account of his plane being badly damaged after a raid on Genshagen near Berlin and his attempt to fly it back to England. As they continued their lone flight towards home, they flew low over the German countryside, making them more vulnerable to ground fire. The B-17, having lost two engines and suffering severe battle damage, was barely able to maintain altitude. Thinking they might not make it back to England, Hibbard activated the bailout bell. The flight engineer, waist and tail gunners, the ball turret gunner, the radio man and the bombardier all jumped. The navigator, Carlton Mendell, was ready to jump when he noticed that the pilot and co-pilot were not making any move to bail out. When he questioned them, they said that they had decided to see if they could make it back.

Hibbard asked him for a heading to an emergency landing field on the English coast. They nursed the plane over the English Channel, setting the plane down successfully on the runways at Beccles, a little-used RAF base on the Suffolk coast.

Our crew, having just returned from a flak leave, a week-long furlough for rest and recreation, was summoned to fly to Beccles and pick up the remaining men. The rest of the story is told in the chapter "Hibbard's Airplane".

What I thought was the end of the story turned out not to be the case. Several months after publishing *An Innocent at Polebrook* I received a letter from James H. Harris of Sonora, California. Having read my book, he informed me that he was on Hibbard's crew as the flight engineer and had bailed out as ordered.

So the story continues. I had always wondered what happened to the crew that bailed out but had no way of attaining information about them. In a series of letters from James Harris I learned much more about what happened to them on that day and the days that followed. It took me over 60 years to learn about this. Following are excerpts from his letters to me:

24 October 2004

Now in answer to your request to share a bit about my imprisonment: My POW days were grim at best. When I was captured by German civilians I was terribly wounded and at that time partially paralyzed. Dragged away and beaten, I was taken with one of the waist gunners to a wooded area where they proceeded to plan our execution by firing squad. The civilian home guard had orders to execute all Air Force personnel while the military had orders to bring us in alive. There was an awful continuing conflict between the two forces throughout the war. Two times the order was given to the ten riflemen to fire and the guns failed to fire. In between the attempted firings the guns were recharged. Just before the last attempt there were 20 shells lying on the ground in random form and I could clearly see the firing pin marks on some of the shells. These were the same guns that they used to shoot at us as we floated to the ground in our parachutes. On the third attempt, as the Burgermeister of the village from whence these people came, framed the word "fire," six soldiers came on the scene and saved us. This was truly a miracle! They knocked the guns down and a terrible battle ensued, with the soldiers winning out when they brought a machine pistol into play. We were hauled off to a military post, then on to the Naval Base at Emden; then to Frankfurt to the Interrogation Center. That was a tough time with my interrogation ending with a bayonet episode.

Then it was on to Stalag Luft IV in Poland. The food allowed us to survive but none to spare. There were 10,000 of us in the four lagers of the prison. The winter of 1944-1945 is the worst in recorded history in Germany. As the Russian armies drove west at lightning speed and came within 11 miles of the camp, we were evacuated. The sick and those who could not walk were taken out by truck and train leaving 1,650 of us to begin what has been called

"The Great Black Death March." We were broken into small groups of about 250 men for much of the march. At night we stayed in barns when available, or slept out in the open.

The freezing weather, deep snow, dysentery, flu, pneumonia and starvation began taking a heavy toll, and over the next 91 days of the march we lost approximately 1,650 men. These men fell by the wayside and I would guess that most of them are still buried in the forests along the country roads and trails we marched on. We were never on main roads or in any cities.

More dead than alive, we marched to the end of the war, covering 550 miles up and down Northern Germany moving slowly west. When liberation came we were so sick and exhausted we hardly realized we were free. There was little exhilaration or excitement.

Then it was on to Belgium and to France. Our evacuation camp was known as Camp Lucky Strike. All of the camps were named after cigarettes. Pieced together a bit and we were on a Liberty ship to South Hampton and then on to Boston. The long train ride to what is now Beale Air Force Base in Yuba City ended with a 90-day furlough. That was a big mistake. It should have been 90 days in the hospital. With so many hundreds and thousands of men returning, hospital beds were a premium and I did not get to one until October. That was the beginning of a major five-year recovery period and beyond, including several surgeries and hospitalizations. I have been for many years 100% disabled. And yet it has been a good life and I have no regrets. It was my duty to serve my country and a very great privilege at the same time.

* * *

4 November 2004

In your PS you mention that you do not understand the bayonet episode. Perhaps I can now place that event in sequence during my Interrogation Center stay.

When we arrived at the Interrogation Center we were immediately photographed, finger printed and given our German dog tags, and then placed in solitary confinement. Our cells were about seven feet long and five feet wide with a bed two feet wide and six feet long. No windows. The walls were painted gray and a 60-watt bulb hung from the ceiling 24 hours a day. A small stool completed the furnishings. A peek hole in the door which opened on to a hall way seemed to be always in use as the guards continually checked on the prisoners. In my case I was treated as a "special prisoner" and had no toilet pot. I was being readied for interrogation on the fuel system of the aircraft. Since I had no pot, I was allowed out of my cell twice a day, or every 12 hours, to use the latrine. Woe to anyone who made a mess in his cell.

Our rations for each day consisted of breakfast that was two and a half ounces of warm water; lunch was the equivalent of a large ice cream scoop of boiled sour barley; and supper was another two and a half ounces of warm water. As you can understand, we did not do well on that kind of diet.

As you can imagine, no medical attention; with walls painted gray; no windows; a bed composed of a burlap sack like mattress filled with wood shavings and supported with wood flats five inches wide but spaced about ten inches apart left one very corrugated; no toilet facilities; a starvation diet; the tension of waiting; the course shouts of the guards the banging and slamming of doors; the constant crunch of the jack booted guards in the hall way; breakdown came rapidly. And if that did not work fast enough other means were employed. . I will not process those thoughts for this time. The Gestapo was resident at the Center as well as in the prison camps.

I do not know how long I was in the interrogation process. It is a complete blank, but I think it was completed within a week. My interrogation began with the usual violence of slamming the cell door open, shouting guards, being dragged down the hall and thrown into the interrogator's large office and ordered to sit in a chair before a large desk. Guards were standing at the doors on the outside, leaving me with the interrogator who made his entrance at the same time. He was a Luftwaffe Colonel.

My interrogation began with a pleasant faced man who went through the formalities and then began to question me about how the outer wing tank fuel was released into the main fuel system. You can guess what kind of answer

I gave. His pleasant demeanor suddenly changed and with screaming language he announced that he knew all about me, and with that he pulled out a large black binder, flipped it open and began to read my history in the Air Force. Every training school I attended was listed. I blurted out what I was thinking. "How do you know this?" His answer was, "You stupid Americans. Our spies have given us all the information we need on every airman." Apparently when one graduated from a training program the base information office would send a story to the local hometown newspaper, and the Germans were collecting that information and sending it back to Germany.

The Colonel was now raging, slamming things around on his desk and he accidentally pushed his telephone onto the floor with a crash and the thing began to ring. At the same time he was yelling at me to tell him what he wanted to know. The commotion was awful what with his screaming, smashing things on his desk, the phone ringing, I believe made the guards think we were in a fight. The doors burst open and a guard charged in with a bayonet on his rifle and came straight for me. I moved as he chased me around the room. Meanwhile the distorted red-faced Colonel was screaming at the guard to get out.

The Colonel had lost his cool for sure and looked like he was about to break down. I believe the Lord intervened here for my interrogation was over and I was shortly moved to a holding area to be shipped to Stalag-Luft IV in Poland. So ended my "bayonet episode."

* * *

20 November 2005

You mentioned in your letter that you wondered about what happened to the bombardier and the other crew members. The bombardier, whose name was Douglas Raymond, was one of the first of the crew to bail out. He used the forward escape hatch. He, like the rest of us, was captured almost immediately. We never saw him again since the officers were separated immediately from the enlisted personnel. He went through interrogation at the Dulag Luft Center near Frankfurt, as all POWs did. From there he was transferred to the Stalag-Luft III at Barth on an inlet from the Baltic Sea. He remained there until the war's end and was an early evacuee to the States. I communicated with him only once. He passed away at an early age and I suppose his imprisonment probably contributed to it. I do not know whether he was wounded or not.

The rest of the enlisted crew, except for a fellow named Hopper Biddle, who had his right arm blown off and who was repatriated through Switzerland back to the States, stayed together throughout our imprisonment, death march and up to the point of our embarkation from Le Havre, France. We were all going to different stateside locations and we left on different ships depending on our physical conditions and release from the hospital. Of course you know about Hibbard, Mendell and our co-pilot Jack Gillam. I hope this will help to answer your questions.

Note: I am indebted to James Harris for his detailed
account of at least a part of his prisoner of war experience.
I know it was difficult for him to divulge these highly
emotional situations and ordeals. He is to be commended
for enduring the horrendous trials he faced, and surviving
them. I feel fortunate that he shared his experiences with
me in his letters and that more people will now get to read
his words. He was a courageous man of great character.
Sadly, James Harris passed away in 2009. In a telephone
conversation with Leslie Goodwin in 2011 I was told that
Harris' widow, Dorothy, was pleased that his story would
be included in this book.

Charles. N. Stevens

From the Navigator's Point of View

As I have indicated before, the navigator, pilot and co-
pilot did not bail out of the plane with the other crewmen.
They nursed the plane back across Germany and the
English Channel, landing at an emergency airstrip at
Beccles on the English coast. The navigator on this flight,
Carlton Mendell, has also written me letters during 2005,
explaining what happened on that flight when the order
was given to bail out.

September 11, 2005

It was the bombardier's duty to take the medical kit to the
rear of the plane and give medicine to the two wounded.
Sometime after the bombardier got to the rear of the plane
Hibbard hit the bail out bell. I waited for the pilot and
co-pilot to go out the nose hatch. After several minutes I

could observe they were still in their seats. I crawled up to talk with them as they as they didn't seem to be in a hurry. It turned out that the experienced co-pilot (20 missions) was trying to convince Hibbard that the two engines left would get us back. When they saw I was still there, they asked me for a heading back to base, which I gave them. It did get us to Beccles on the coast.

September 26, 2005

Some of the gunners and the bombardier were disturbed by Hibbard's 'hasty bail out bell.' What went on between Hibbard and the co-pilot was a decision to fly the plane home. My course back was predicated on wisdom from previous navigators who said, if you come back from a mission alone and cannot find your position on a map, take a mag. heading of 270 degrees and you would make landfall somewhere on the British coast.

Final Note:

Sadly, Howard Hibbard, piloting a B-17G, was killed in a crash on June 8, 1945. Apparently the plane was heading home when it plowed into a hillside, Craig Cwn Llwyd, near Valley, Wales in bad weather. Our original ball turret gunner, the one who was severely injured by flak on our third mission (Hamburg, Germany) was also killed in the same crash. Also a victim of that tragedy was the weatherman who played our little G.I. organ at our church services. Twenty men, a full crew and ten passengers, died in the crash. Their stone crosses stand in the American Cemetery at Mattingly, near Cambridge.

Parachutes at Augsburg

I wrote about a raid to Augsburg, Germany that occurred on July 19, 1944 in my previous book, *An Innocent at Polebrook*. The chapter was titled "A First Encounter." Our group was nearing the target, the Messerschmitt Aircraft Factory, when a half dozen FW-190s attacked us. On a single pass the fighters shot down two of our bombers, one exploding, the other falling in a spin. Only two parachutes opened. I saw none of this because they attacked us from the rear while I was facing forward. Except for feeling sad about the lost crew members and hope for the two who had managed to bail out, I thought that was the end of the story.

Within the past year I have met Dennis C. Lord whose mother's first husband was a crew member on one of those ill-fated planes. Unfortunately he went down with the plane. Becoming interested in that incident, Lord also wondered about the fate of the two crew members who had bailed out. Through dogged research and effort he discovered that one of the men who had jumped, Sgt. Charles Wiles, the Flight Engineer on the crew, was living in Orlando, Florida. Lord contacted him and visited in his home, learning first hand about what happened on that terrible afternoon in 1944.

After having trouble leaving the ship and having even more difficulty with his parachute, Wiles landed in a field. A German soldier and a farmer with a pitchfork met him as he came down. He was taken to Frankfurt for interrogation then spent the rest of the war as a POW in a Stalag Luft. As the Russians advanced from the east, the guards fled, and the prisoners were urged to go west until they found the American lines. This became the famous Death March during which many men perished. Wiles is one of the survivors.

On March 19, 2011 Dennis Lord spoke at the Western Museum of Flight in Torrance, California, his main subject the above incident on the Augsburg mission. When he finished his presentation, he introduced Charles Wiles whom he had arranged to fly from Orlando. I, having been invited to attend the talk, was able to meet the fellow airman from the 351st Bomb Group.

Short and slender, with wavy white hair, he is clearly not used to notoriety or being the center of attention. I was able to talk to him only briefly. I wondered how he felt floating down in his parachute, watching all of us go on without him. The feeling was inexpressible. "You know," said Wiles, "when I landed in that field, they took me into a farmhouse. The woman of the house asked me in broken English where I was from. I said Rochester,

New York. She said I once lived in Rochester too." Both were surprised.

Asked to speak at the presentation, he could say only, and with obvious emotion, "I lost a lot of good friends that day." I was lucky enough to survive 34 bombing missions and still have some ghastly pictures in my head, but they pale compared to the pictures that that must reside in his.

Hanging Around B-17s

When the B-17s visit California in the springtime, my wife and I are usually there with them, answering questions about the B-17 during wartime and offering my books for sale. Many people, who come out for a flight or a tour of the plane, are very interested in World War II, especially the 8th Air Force and the strategic bombing of Germany. Sales of my books, *An Innocent at Polebrook* and *The Innocent Cadet* are usually brisk.

I attempt to answer the many questions that people ask and address some of their misconceptions. Most of their knowledge comes from veterans they knew, books and especially movies, notably "Twelve O'clock High" and "The Memphis Belle."

Other than the standard questions about how high we flew, how long our missions were and how many bombs we could carry, the most frequent query is about how many missions we flew. Almost everyone believes that 25 missions was the standard tour. This idea came from the movie "The Memphis Belle." I have to explain that 25 missions was indeed a tour at one time, but was extended as conditions improved to 30 then 35 missions. I tell them about my own experience when 30 missions was considered a tour, but was told at the end of my 29th mission that I now had to complete 35.

The second most asked question is, "Is it true that the bombardier has control of the plane on the bomb run?" Yes, I tell them, through the Norden bombsight (most call it the "Norton" bombsight) and the auto-pilot, the bombardier guides the plane. They also believe that every bombardier in every plane has a bombsight. I have to tell them that out of a squadron of twelve bombers only one or two would carry a bombsight, the rest dropping when the lead plane drops. Many trained bombardiers never used a bombsight.

The visitors to the B-17s are overwhelmingly interested in having their questions answered and always thank me for my service. When they thank me, they are thanking all veterans. The veterans of World War II are genuinely revered by the general public.

Those who tour the B-17s, entering by way of a ladder through the nose hatch and exiting through the waist door, are amazed at how small and confined it is. Some say it is almost claustrophobic. People are used to flying in modern, wide-bodied jets, so their idea of space is different from what ours was then. I always thought it was quite roomy.

They are also astounded about how basic the bomber is inside, its bare, skeletal look devoid of any comforts found in modern planes. They comment about the narrow footing across the bomb bay and the effort of squeezing through the two struts that support it. But we were slim and trim in those days, and the narrowness did not bother us. One portly man ripped the buttons off his shirt as he squeezed through the struts, tearing it at the same time. He emerged in his undershirt, carrying his ripped shirt.

Sometimes the lines of people waiting to tour the plane are over 100 feet long, some waiting for over an hour for their chance to go through it. I am amazed at how much interest there is in a relic from World War II.

Those who take a flight in the B-17 at over $400 each are thrilled. Some say it is the supreme experience in their lives. All are more than satisfied, smiles on their faces as they walk away. Even though they don't fly very high or far, don't have to wear oxygen masks or fly through any flak, they get a sense of what it was like for us and an appreciation for what the airmen went though. A typical comment is, "I loved the flight, but I can't imagine going on a bombing mission like you did. I don't think I could do it."

Three B-17s make tours of the United States during the spring and summer. They are the "Liberty Belle" owned by the Liberty Belle Foundation, the "Aluminum Overcast" owned by the Experimental Aircraft Association (EAA) and the "Nine-O-Nine" owned by the Collings Foundation. The latter also flies a B-24 and a P-51. Each organization has a website listing its schedules.

I must say that the owners, schedulers, sales people, mechanics and pilots have been very kind in allowing

Dolores and me to become a small part of their group as they swing through California and Arizona.

I admit that I still love to hang around B-17s. They were part of such a pivotal period in my life. I still admire the way it looks, poised and powerful on the tarmac. I like the way it sounds, the distinctive throbbing of its engines, even the squeal of its brakes as it taxies. I thrill at the sight of it taking off, rising slowly as it retracts its landing gear, flying off for a mission into the future.

About the Author

Charles N. Stevens, or Norm as his friends call him, grew up in Inglewood, California. At 18 he joined the Army Air Corps. He entered in 1943 and was discharged after the war in October 1945. He served as a bombardier on a B-17 in the 8th Air Force, 351st Bomb Group, at Polebrook, England during the summer and early fall of 1944. He finished his tour of duty, completing 34 bombing missions over Germany and occupied France, Belgium and Holland.

He wrote extensively about his combat experiences in his previous book, *An Innocent at Polebrook: A Memoir of an 8th Air Force Bombardier*, published in 2004. His second book was a prequel detailing his year of training before going overseas, *The Innocent Cadet: Becoming a World War II Bombardier*, published in 2008.

After returning from overseas he trained as a radar bombardier at Langley Field, Virginia and Williams Field, Arizona. He was to be assigned to a B-29 crew for duty in the Pacific when the war ended.

Following the war he enrolled at the University of California at Los Angeles, graduating with a BA in psychology. After a series of graduate courses he earned his teaching credential. Over a span of 32 years he taught science and mathematics in junior high schools and English and American Literature in high school. While teaching he earned a master's degree in English at California State College at Los Angles.

He has two sons by a previous marriage, Jeffry L. Stevens and Greg E. Stevens. He has five grandchildren, Brenda Stevens Sherry, Eric, Sharon, Michael and Beth Stevens, and two great grandsons, Ryan and Colin Stevens.

He retired in 1984 and has lived a life of reading, writing, traveling and being a grandfather. He lives with his wife, Dolores Seidman, in Monterey Park, California where they have resided for 40 years.